Northern Ireland: A Very Short Introduction

VERY SHORT INTRODUCTIONS are for anyone wanting a stimulating and accessible way into a new subject. They are written by experts, and have been translated into more than 45 different languages.

The series began in 1995, and now covers a wide variety of topics in every discipline. The VSI library currently contains over 600 volumes—a Very Short Introduction to everything from Psychology and Philosophy of Science to American History and Relativity—and continues to grow in every subject area.

Very Short Introductions available now:

ABOLITIONISM Richard S. Newman
THE ABRAHAMIC RELIGIONS
    Charles L. Cohen
ACCOUNTING Christopher Nobes
ADAM SMITH Christopher J. Berry
ADOLESCENCE Peter K. Smith
ADVERTISING Winston Fletcher
AERIAL WARFARE Frank Ledwidge
AESTHETICS Bence Nanay
AFRICAN AMERICAN RELIGION
    Eddie S. Glaude Jr
AFRICAN HISTORY John Parker and
    Richard Rathbone
AFRICAN POLITICS Ian Taylor
AFRICAN RELIGIONS
    Jacob K. Olupona
AGEING Nancy A. Pachana
AGNOSTICISM Robin Le Poidevin
AGRICULTURE Paul Brassley and
    Richard Soffe
ALBERT CAMUS Oliver Gloag
ALEXANDER THE GREAT
    Hugh Bowden
ALGEBRA Peter M. Higgins
AMERICAN CULTURAL HISTORY
    Eric Avila
AMERICAN FOREIGN RELATIONS
    Andrew Preston
AMERICAN HISTORY Paul S. Boyer
AMERICAN IMMIGRATION
    David A. Gerber
AMERICAN LEGAL HISTORY
    G. Edward White
AMERICAN NAVAL HISTORY
    Craig L. Symonds

AMERICAN POLITICAL HISTORY
    Donald Critchlow
AMERICAN POLITICAL PARTIES
    AND ELECTIONS L. Sandy Maisel
AMERICAN POLITICS Richard M. Valelly
THE AMERICAN PRESIDENCY
    Charles O. Jones
THE AMERICAN REVOLUTION
    Robert J. Allison
AMERICAN SLAVERY
    Heather Andrea Williams
THE AMERICAN WEST Stephen Aron
AMERICAN WOMEN'S HISTORY
    Susan Ware
ANAESTHESIA Aidan O'Donnell
ANALYTIC PHILOSOPHY
    Michael Beaney
ANARCHISM Colin Ward
ANCIENT ASSYRIA Karen Radner
ANCIENT EGYPT Ian Shaw
ANCIENT EGYPTIAN ART AND
    ARCHITECTURE Christina Riggs
ANCIENT GREECE Paul Cartledge
THE ANCIENT NEAR EAST
    Amanda H. Podany
ANCIENT PHILOSOPHY Julia Annas
ANCIENT WARFARE Harry Sidebottom
ANGELS David Albert Jones
ANGLICANISM Mark Chapman
THE ANGLO-SAXON AGE John Blair
ANIMAL BEHAVIOUR
    Tristram D. Wyatt
THE ANIMAL KINGDOM
    Peter Holland
ANIMAL RIGHTS David DeGrazia

Available soon:

For more information visit our website

www.oup.com/vsi/

Marc Mulholland

NORTHERN IRELAND

A Very Short Introduction

SECOND EDITION

OXFORD
UNIVERSITY PRESS

OXFORD
UNIVERSITY PRESS

Great Clarendon Street, Oxford, OX2 6DP,
United Kingdom

Oxford University Press is a department of the University of Oxford.
It furthers the University's objective of excellence in research, scholarship,
and education by publishing worldwide. Oxford is a registered trade mark of
Oxford University Press in the UK and in certain other countries

First edition published 2003
Second edition published 2020

Impression: 3

Published in the United States of America by Oxford University Press
198 Madison Avenue, New York, NY 10016, United States of America

British Library Cataloguing in Publication Data

Data available

Library of Congress Control Number: 2020930607

ISBN 978-0-19-882500-5

Printed and bound by
CPI Group (UK) Ltd, Croydon, CR0 4YY

Contents

List of illustrations

The publisher and author have made every effort to trace and contact all copyright holders before publication. If notified, the publisher will be pleased to rectify any errors or omissions at the earliest opportunity.

Northern Ireland

Introduction

More than 3,500 people died in the Northern Ireland Troubles, conventionally dated between 1968 and 1998. An ocean of misery for those directly affected it was nonetheless a small-scale conflict. By the standards of the two parameters which might be considered especially relevant—the catastrophic European 20th century and the bloody and vicious Cold War—the Troubles were a grim footnote. This does little to detract from the political and psychological interest of Northern Ireland, particularly in the Global North. Because it was English-speaking, usually hospitable to journalists, amply provided for by sophisticated agencies of data collection, and also, it seems likely, because it was overwhelmingly white, the conflict in Northern Ireland garnered an intensity of Western observation that more ravaged parts of the world could only dream of. The Troubles must be unique in an armed conflict in having its every victim of legal violence recorded and named (not least in that memorial of dignified scholarship *Lost Lives*, published in 1999). Northern Ireland is a community of people and needs to be understood as that. It is also a case study of civil conflict and peace building.

Northern Ireland is a good example of what psychologists call 'social identity'. There seems to be a human instinct, arising from our nature as a cooperative species, to adopt group allegiances which burrow deep into our personalities. We may identify with the political party, a social class, a town, a sport, a nation, even a supranational identity. Sometimes these identities, rather than cross-cutting, mutually reinforce one another so that multiple group identities congeal into one stark divide. Northern Ireland would seem to be one such case. Catholics and Protestants in Northern Ireland were, and are, particularly adept at 'telling', a term psychologists use for the art of working out the background of a stranger by linguistic, phonetic, and visual indicators. 'You treat everyone as an Orangee until you know different,' as one youth told Frank Burton, a social anthropologist; and vice versa.

In Northern Ireland strong views exist. One survey carried out by the psychologist E. E. O'Donnell in the 1970s found that the 'stereotype that Protestants have of Roman Catholics is that they are ordinary enough people, but Irish-nationalist-republican. They are seen as brain-washed by priests, having too many children, and as being superstitious and bitter. Roman Catholics, on the other hand, think Protestants are in control of the country and are determined to remain in control, even at the cost of bitter murder. This is because they are seen to be loyal Orangemen.' Leaving aside deprecatory language, it is difficult to say that these stereotypes were drastically inaccurate. It was not a matter of two communities misunderstanding each other, rather they understood each other rather well: but they disagreed about the very nature of the dispute. For Catholics, the conflict was essentially about nationality, for Protestants, it was essentially about religion. As Richard Rose put it in 1971, 'Because Catholics see discord in nationality terms whereas Protestants see it in religious terms, politics in Northern Ireland involves ideologically unrelated conflict.'

The Northern Ireland conflict, therefore, was never entirely symmetrical. It was not simply a matter of two communities facing off, but rather a dispute about how the issues at conflict were to be defined and managed. This means that the British government, in particular, was always a crucial active agent, one which saw itself as above the fray but in so doing was deluded about its own interests, prejudices, and motivations. The Northern Irish had their own stereotype of 'perfidious Albion', again not entirely inaccurate. As Raymond McClean, a Derry doctor, put it, 'the sin of the Englishman was a complicated, inherent hypocrisy, often unbeknownst to himself'. To Catholic and Protestant alike, the British often appeared smug, self-righteous, and aggravatingly blind to their own faults. Britain, it seemed, gave itself a licence to break its own proudly advertised norms. The Northern Ireland Troubles should be seen as a tripartite contest. Certainly, the peace which has been built and continues to be built upon relies on this truth.

This second edition of the *Northern Ireland Very Short Introduction* has been completely rewritten. It has been reduced in length while including material on the first two decades of the 21st century which necessarily did not feature in the first edition. I have tried to reflect the evolution of my own thinking on the Troubles as informed by a robust and lively scholarship. If any reader were to compare the two editions, they would find somewhat greater attention paid here to women. While I have tried throughout to make the sequence of events in Northern Ireland clear this edition pays somewhat more attention to themes and concepts.

This short book has been written during the Brexit crisis, which to an unprecedented degree has flung Northern Ireland to the forefront of UK-wide political calculations. Since the Good Friday Agreement of 1998, both nationalists and unionists had broadly agreed that the constitutional status quo would remain in place for the foreseeable future. Brexit drastically upset the balance. In a poll carried out by Lord Ashcroft's company in September 2019, 51 per cent of respondents in Northern Ireland, once the 'Don't Knows' were excluded, indicated that they would vote for a United Ireland. This was an outlier poll, certainly, but its significance was clear. The sands in Northern Ireland were shifting.

Chapter 1
The origins of the Troubles

The conflict in Northern Ireland had long roots though we must be careful not to conclude from this that it was simply a throwback to the past. It was the product of the collision of two groups and, over the long span of time, involved much more peaceful coexistence than active conflict. This was never, however, particularly happy cohabitation.

Ulster in the North of Ireland, six counties of which make up modern Northern Ireland (Antrim, Armagh, Down, Fermanagh, Londonderry, and Tyrone), long had close connections with independent Scotland. For centuries, this had helped protect it from the control of the English Crown and Ulster was the most stoutly 'Gaelic' of the Irish provinces. The success of militant Reformation in Scotland from 1560, in contrast to the English failure to effectively impose mass Protestant conversion on Ireland, broke the United Ulster–Scottish Gaelic front. In a bloody war of conquest, which reached near genocidal proportions, Elizabethan England conquered and laid waste to Catholic Gaelic Ulster between 1593 and 1603.

The heartland of counties Antrim and Down, meanwhile, absorbed large-scale migration from across the Irish Sea. This area was ringed by a government-organized 'plantation' of settlers from across Great Britain beginning in 1609. Ulster became a stronghold of Irish Protestantism, where Presbyterians of Scottish origin were uniquely numerous. Catholics, many of them still thinking of themselves as Gaelic, were not extirpated, however. Creating landholding patterns that still obtain, they were moved to poorer uplands and town outskirts beyond the walls. Bitterness between settler and native ran deep with all the additional venom of religious conflict. In 1641 a Catholic rebellion led to the massacre of Protestant settlers, though interestingly Scottish Presbyterians were left relatively untouched. The rebellion was eventually crushed but insurgent atrocities, which lost nothing in the retelling, became part of the Protestant collective memory.

In 1690, the plantation town of Londonderry stood siege against the largely Catholic army of King James II, recently ousted from the English throne by 'William of Orange' in the Glorious Revolution. The 'apprentice boys', heroic plebeians of the town, had forced the gates shut against the protests of Londonderry's governor, Lundy. Well into the 19th century, the Siege of Derry was a widely honoured part of 'this island story' across the Protestant British Isles. It was an intrinsic part of the British mythology. In the 20th century, William III, the Protestant king, was a commonplace on Orange Order banners and on gable walls. Every 1 December an effigy of 'Lundy', the eternal traitor, would be burnt in Londonderry.

Tensions remained between Presbyterians and the established Protestant church throughout the 18th century, however. Presbyterians were formally discriminated against, if not quite to the same extent as Catholics. Ulster Scots emigrated to America in droves, and were leading forces in the American drive for independence. Ulster was inspired particularly by the French revolution, and many Presbyterians raised the banner of ultra-radical republicanism and Irish separatism in the 1790s. They were the Ulster mainstay of the revolutionary United Irishmen. The movement was not powerful enough to overcome the Crown and the 1798 rebellion was crushed. The inspiration of separatist republicanism, however, was sufficient to mobilize Catholics from their crushed torpor and to equip them with a cohesive and largely democratic ideology of nationalism. Ulster Protestants, including even the Presbyterians, increasingly saw the clear and present danger to their civil, political, and religious liberties coming now not from England, but from the rising Catholic Irish majority. They feared that majority rule in Ireland would mean domination by the oppressive morality of the Roman Catholic Church.

In 1801 the old Irish Protestant Parliament was abolished, and Irish representation was integrated into the United Kingdom Parliament. This should have squared the circle, by allowing Catholic representation in a securely majority Protestant Parliament. British anti-Catholicism, however, delayed this outcome until it was wrested from Westminster in 1829, by the first mass civil rights movement in Ireland led by Daniel O'Connell. The Orange Order, established in Ulster in 1798 as a counter-revolutionary movement of Church of Ireland tenant farmers, had at first opposed the Union abolishing the separate Irish Parliament as an infringement of Protestant rights. After emancipation, it seemed to Orange Protestants that the Union was the principal protection against the prospect of an overbearing Catholic democracy.

Protestant Ulster had further reason to distinguish itself from the Catholic nationalism that was becoming the common sense of majority Irish public opinion. Its culture—doughty, self-reliant, energetic, and indifferent to aristocratic affectation—made for economic prosperity and an impressive capitalist ethic. If 19th-century Ireland took its tone from the beleaguered and defiant peasantry, 19th-century Ulster took its spirit from the industrious self-improving farmer, artisan, and entrepreneur. First the linen industry spread, then, in particular from the 1840s, marine industry. In 1842, the English author William Thackeray took the 'Newry Lark' coach from Dundalk, heading for Belfast through Portadown and Armagh. He was immediately struck by the difference he saw as he travelled into Ulster:

> At any rate, it is clear that the towns are vastly improved, the cottages and villages no less so; the people look active and well dressed; a sort of weight seems to be taken all at once from the Englishman's mind on entering the province, when he finds himself once more looking upon comfort and activity and resolution. What is the cause of this improvement? Protestantism is...but for Protestantism would it not be as well to read Scotchism?—meaning thrift, prudence, perseverance, boldness, and common sense.

Self-confident Protestant evangelism, however, was not well adapted to winning over Catholics, or even encouraging much by way of cooperative ecumenism. Ulster Protestantism seemed best when it stood alone, contributing to the United Kingdom rather than abjectly depending upon London or deferring to Dublin. The catastrophic famine of 1845 to 1850, which ravaged the South, more or less left Protestant Ulster untouched, at least insofar as few died of actual starvation. In all, godly providence seemed to favour the Protestant North.

Partition

It should be borne in mind, however, that Irish unionism was not yet a partitionist ideology. As an organized political force, it emerged as a reaction to the Irish nationalist challenge. A parliamentary Home Rule party had emerged with Catholic support in the 1870s. Home Rule was another name for a devolved parliament and government with limited powers over domestic affairs. Under this proposed scheme, Ireland would remain part of the United Kingdom and its foreign policy under British control. Though far short of actual independence, it was felt in Ireland that this was as far as the nationalist claims could realistically be pushed at the time.

From the outset, unionists were suspicious that any such
Parliament must eventually move towards the direction of
outright separation from the United Kingdom. Between 1879 and
1881, Charles Stewart Parnell MP, himself a Protestant, combined
with the radical Land League in a militant campaign for the
abolition of landlordism and in favour of small farmers owning
their own land. This relied mostly upon the 'boycott', the economic
isolation and ruination of Land League enemies. Behind it stood
the 'moonlighters', armed peasant vigilantes prepared to use
violence (Figure 1). Something like seventy-nine people died in
this Land War. The landed gentry specifically, and many
Protestants in general, saw the lash-up between Home Rule and
the semi-revolutionary Land League as a fearful portend for the
future. It upended liberal norms regarding the security of property
and showed mobilized Catholic democracy, in Protestant eyes, as
oppressively majoritarian and intolerant of minorities. An
underground revolutionary republican organization (the 'Fenians')

1. 'Moonlighters', Irish rural vigilantes who fought landlordism in the
1880s, depicted in a comic print. Colloquially they were known as 'the
boys', a term also used for the IRA in the Northern Ireland Troubles.
Extra-legal political violence has a long tradition in Ireland.

had been in existence since 1858. In 1888 its American wing gave welcome to the prospect of a Home Rule Parliament as a step towards separatist revolution. 'The achievement of a National Parliament gives us a footing upon Irish soil: it...gives us what we may well express as the plant of an armed revolution.' What the Fenians hoped for, the unionists feared.

In 1885, an 'Ulster Party' of Unionist MPs, itself dominated by landlords, formed as an autonomous parliamentary political party. The following year, the British Prime Minister, Gladstone, came out in favour of Home Rule, though his measure was defeated, mostly by English political opinion. Irish unionism was vocal and effective in the debate. It was dominated by the mostly southern-based Irish landed elite. Though the Irish gentry lacked a democratic mandate compared to the solid phalanx of Unionist voters in Ulster, they had all-important social and cultural capital that gifted them enormous influence with the political ruling class of England. Particularly as they brought the prosperous Protestant bourgeoisie behind them, unionists could convincingly present themselves as the quality of Ireland, having much in common with the best of Victorian values. Mass unionism in Ulster, on the other hand, became strongly associated with rancorous Orangism, bigotry, and sectarian violence. Serious rioting by the Belfast working classes in 1886, sparked by the first Home Rule bill, may have been successful in reinforcing British certainty that Irish self-government would be a debacle, but it was by no means an advertisement for the civility of Ulster unionism. At least until the establishment of the Ulster Unionist Council in 1905, therefore, Irish unionism was an all-Ireland affair, under the leadership of an all-Ireland elite.

This encouraged amongst nationalists the tenacious idea that Irish and even Ulster unionism was essentially fragile. Nationalists saw themselves as welded together by a long and self-sacrificing struggle against enormous odds for Irish self-determination. In contrast, unionism appeared to be an unstable amalgam lumping together the class privileges of the landed elite, the narrow materialism of the business classes (who, they joked, were 'more loyal to the half-crown rather than to the Crown'), and the Orange bigotry of Protestant workers in the North. They were convinced that the class and even religious tensions within the Unionist bloc—for Presbyterians and the Church of Ireland never quite saw eye to eye—were only held together by the supportive framework of British political interest. It was a favourite rhetorical ploy of nationalists to quote Randolph Churchill in 1886, when he cynically declared his willingness to 'play the Orange card' simply to discomfort his political rival, William Gladstone. Once insincere guarantees of support were withdrawn by selfish British politicians, nationalists were convinced, unionism would fall apart, and the older 18th-century traditions of Protestant patriotism would re-emerge.

Unionists, for their part, believed that only a multinational United Kingdom could resist Catholic ascendancy within Ireland and retain civil, political, and religious freedom for all. Unionism was designed to save Ireland from fatal division. Even as democratic ideas became more powerful in the political mainstream and resistance to the third Home Rule bill of 1912 centred upon Ulster where a Unionist electoral majority existed, its leadership lay with Sir Edward Carson, a Dublin lawyer. The 1912 Ulster Covenant, signed by 500,000 people, warned that in the event of Home Rule being imposed upon Ireland, the nine counties of Ulster (rather than the six counties which would eventually make up Northern Ireland) would establish their own Provisional Government. Even this, however, was calculated as a measure to frustrate Home Rule for the entire island. And when Unionist negotiators considered the possibility of the formal exclusion of Ulster, or a part of it, from the provisions of the Home Rule bill, the animating idea was still the same: to sabotage Home Rule as a whole. The Unionist hope was that Irish nationalist leaders would never accept partition as a price for limited self-government.

When Unionists began to broach the possibility of partition in 1914, it was still as a means to sabotage Home Rule. However, the prospect of Protestant Ulster cutting itself off entirely from disloyal Ireland was growing in popularity amongst the Protestants of the North. Carson's Ulster lieutenants, notably James Craig, were growing tired of incessant agitation from the South. For many, the republican and separatist Easter Rebellion of 1916 in Dublin was the last straw. The old southern Irish Unionist leadership was still powerful, however, with members sitting in the British War Cabinet, and they were primarily responsible for frustrating attempts at an emergency all-Ireland Home Rule settlement in the latter half of 1916. By 1917, as republican separatism grew in strength in southern Ireland, they realized their mistake.

Irish nationalism had accepted the compromise of Home Rule only so long as it seemed that deference to the British Imperial Crown was a minor, if aggravating, inconvenience. It seemed a price well worth paying for winning support for Home Rule in liberal Britain and to placate Ulster unionist objections. Once it became clear, however, that much of Ulster was likely to be excluded from the jurisdiction of an Irish Home Rule Parliament, its attractiveness diminished drastically. On top of this, participation in the First World War signalled that forced inclusion in the Empire was hardly cost free. Republican hardliners, many of whom had tolerated the idea of Home Rule as a step in the right direction, were now convinced that it would be shameful for Irish nationalists to fight in British uniform against Germany while refusing to strike a blow for their own freedom. A small minority carried out the Easter insurrection of 1916. They were crushed, but as the smoke cleared republican separatism won the respect and increasingly the fervent support of Catholic Ireland. Sinn Féin, founded as a political party in 1906, became a mass formation committed to an independent Irish Republic in 1917. It won virtually every nationalist seat in the 1918 general election and in 1919 its elected representatives, rather than take their seats at Westminster, established Dáil Eireann in Dublin, an independent parliament and government. It promptly declared Ireland independent.

Impressively comprehensive though Sinn Féin's democratic clearly was, at least outside Ulster, imperialist Britain was in no mind to accept it. The Irish Volunteers, who saw themselves as the army of the Irish government, evolved into the Irish Republican Army (IRA). From 1919, the IRA stumbled across guerrilla warfare as the classic 'national liberation' method of struggle against overwhelming military force. Confronted by the crisis, Ulster unionism was now determined to secure the Union where it could, in the six north-east counties of Ulster which combined a fairly safe Protestant majority of two-thirds with the largest practicable extent of territory. The 1920 Government of Ireland Act set up a Northern Ireland Parliament and government, which came into power the following year. Ironically, Home Rule had come to north-east Ulster.

The substantial Catholic and nationalist minority in this new Northern Ireland at first hoped that partition would be only temporary. Two nationalist-controlled local authorities refused allegiance to the new Northern Ireland state. But it soon became clear that no compromise could be effected between North and South. The 1921 treaty between Britain and Ireland included agreement on a process for readjusting the border, to the disgruntlement of Ulster Unionists. Nationalists fondly hoped that this would make Northern Ireland unviable but as it turned out the adjustments proposed were minor and the boundary was left as it had been. Northern Ireland, with its own devolved government, was firmly fixed in the United Kingdom.

Unionists had always made much of the argument that the economic success of north-east Ulster proved the superiority of their culture. Indeed, Belfast and the surrounding area was a major industrial centre in the 19th and early 20th century

2. Industrial Belfast in the mid-20th century. Unionists justifiably took pride in Ulster's industrial heritage. Deindustrialization at the end of the 20th century was traumatic for the Protestant working-class community.

(Figure 2). It boasted the largest and the third largest shipyards in the world, as well as an enormous marine and textile industry ('Irish linen' as it was always advertised, rather than 'Ulster linen'). As it happened, the crisis of Northern Ireland's heavy industry virtually coincided with the act of partition. Unemployment soared and stayed vertiginously high until well into the Second World War. The scrabble for jobs added a bitterness to the early 1920s Troubles, when the IRA fought the fledgling institutions of the state: the Royal Ulster Constabulary (RUC) and the entirely Protestant police reserve, the Specials. Catholics and left-wing Protestant workers were evicted by fellow-workers from their jobs, and nationalist streets were burnt out by loyalist mobs. Even as the convulsive violence petered out in 1922, the Northern Ireland economy continued to struggle throughout the interwar period. Catholics in Northern Ireland sourly accepted that partition would remain in place for the foreseeable future, but they were in no mood for generous accommodation.

The Northern Ireland Parliament and government, relocated to the grandiloquent Stormont building in 1932, did nothing to ameliorate division. Stormont had only the limited powers of a devolved government and in exchange for British Exchequer support for its rickety finances it declined to pull those few economic levers that might have increased the region's competitiveness vis-à-vis Great Britain. The outcome was a parliamentary arena centred not upon questions of economic growth and distribution, which might have encouraged class alignments cutting across the religious and national divide, but rather a myopic and repetitive concentration on the symbolism of the 'border question'. Devolution, therefore, helped perpetuate a politics of culture-war which could be freely indulged in by an otherwise trumpery administration. Irish nationalists often refused to turn up at Stormont and when they did were neither invited nor minded to participate constructively.

The Northern Ireland state

Northern Ireland was established as a means to preserve as much of Ireland as possible for the Union. Any development toward something further than that, an Ulster nationalism, was weak indeed. Home Rule in Ireland was not a second-order kind of independence or a transition to the 'real thing', as it certainly would have been in Ireland as a whole, but rather a bulwark and defence against threats to the Union. With no incentive to create a national democracy Unionist politicians such as the first three Prime Ministers—James Craig, John Andrews, and Basil Brooke—saw no advantage and only risk in seeking to draw the Catholic minority into the new political dispensation. In effect, all Catholics were seen as an Irish nationalist fifth column, and it was better to have them clearly defined as such and out in the open. It is perhaps unlikely that any substantial Catholic loyalism would ever have been forthcoming, but certainly no attempt was made to develop it. A militant Orange culture pervaded the institutions of state. The 12th of July, when Orange Lodges marched through the streets to commemorate William III and the institution of Protestant ascendancy, was a state holiday. When the Prince of Wales visited to open Stormont there was an honour guard of 5,000 Orangemen. Unionists were broadly encouraged to maintain a soft boycott of Catholic institutions. In the 1940s, as Benedict Kiely recorded, the Orange Order issued a pamphlet in which it was warned 'That any member of the Orange Institution found frequenting Roman Catholic public-houses is guilty of conduct unbecoming an Orangeman'.

Nonetheless, this was not simple triumphalism. Unionists were forever anxious. They were well aware that the British government had tried to push them to accept a level of subordination to the new Dublin government in 1921, admittedly as an attempt to keep the concentric circles of Ireland within the ambit of the British Empire. Unionists were all too well aware that attempts could be made to sell their interests again. In 1939, British Prime Minister Neville Chamberlain once more put pressure on the Stormont government to accept post-war inclusion in a United Ireland as a temptation for the government led by Eamon de Valera in Dublin to join the war against Germany. This came to nothing, southern Ireland remaining neutral, but for Unionists the risk was all too clear.

On the face of it, the unionist majority in Northern Ireland seemed safe enough. The Catholic population of Northern Ireland in 1926 was only 33.5 per cent, down from 39.5 per cent in 1911. The risk, however, was that if partition seemed to fade as a pressing question of the day the Unionist electoral alliance might well break up along class and perhaps denominational lines. The governing Ulster Unionist Party feared the prospect of left-wing candidates allying Catholic and Protestant voters to steal seats here, or ultra-Protestant candidates splitting the vote there. In a worst-case scenario, Unionist control of Stormont might be lost or simply weakened, and an unsympathetic British government would see this as an excuse to renegotiate the Irish settlement in its entirety. As the Nationalist Party leader, Cahir Healy, pointed out in 1934, Unionist loyalty was much more to their own position than it was to any possible future British government:

> The King governs through his Ministers, and the Administration here does not know the day when a Socialist Government may replace the National one [at Westminster], so they stipulate for a conditional loyalty to the Throne, just so long as it suits.

The Unionist Party and government, therefore, worked to maintain a balance which would preserve both the hegemonic unionist bloc and a subordinate but clearly demarcated nationalist bloc. Gerrymandering—the drawing of constituency boundaries to corral nationalist and unionist votes—was designed not to eliminate nationalist representation, but to peg it permanently into a minority role. Border areas, however, which tended to be strongly Catholic, had to be held for the Union if questions were not to be raised about the logic of the partition line. Londonderry in particular, as the second city and a key part of unionist mythology, had to be kept under Unionist control despite its Catholic majority.

In 1967 there were a total of seventy-three separate local authorities; only ten of these were controlled by non-Unionists. In twelve local government areas which had a Catholic majority in the population there was a Protestant/Unionist majority in the Council. Local authorities were important because they had a significant role in the distribution of public housing. But they should be seen as only one part of an overall structure of segregation. As the official 'Macrory Report' on local government issued in May 1970 observed:

> The Roman Catholic population—over 35 per cent—is not only in a permanent minority at Stormont—never securing more than one quarter of the seats in the House of Commons—but at present controls one in seven local authorities and none above the level of

an Urban District Council. Nor has there emerged in the local councils with Unionist majorities—with very few exceptions (e.g. Ballymena)—a disposition to share even the humblest municipal offices with the Catholics.

On top of this, it was seen as necessary to conserve jobs for Protestants if the lower Protestant emigration rate that counterbalanced the higher Catholic birth rate was to be maintained (by one calculation, by Denis Barritt and Charles F. Carter, the Catholic one-third of the population gave rise to about 55–8 per cent of total emigration). A complex interweaving of gerrymandering, a property franchise in local government elections, and discrimination in private and public employment all combined to structurally underpin a relatively precarious Unionist dominance. This was never admitted publicly but was common knowledge. A Protestant minister in Derry in the 1950s, Victor Griffin, remembered,

> Protestants pressed would admit to discrimination against Roman Catholics, particularly in employment, but they were justified on the grounds that the Church of Rome was intent on destroying the State and having a United Ireland under Roman rule. Therefore giving influential jobs... to followers of the Pope would mean placing potential traitors in positions of power.

Those Catholics employed in private industry were considered to be there only on sufferance. As one pro-Unionist writer, William Caron, put it, rather threateningly, 'it may suffice to say that the great majority of large industrial concerns in Ulster were built up and owned by Protestants: if they were to disappear, some eighty per cent of the Roman Catholic population would be out of work.' During the first half of the 20th century, the condition of Belfast Catholics actually declined. They became more concentrated in unskilled work while Protestants tightened their grip on skilled positions and public and professional occupations. A nadir was reached in 1951. Expansion in industries such as construction and so-called 'sheltered' white-collar occupations like education began to improve the position of Catholics thereafter. Nonetheless, in 1971 Catholics were still two and a half times more likely to be unemployed than Protestants.

Reform and 'revolution'

Unionist Northern Ireland had a good world war. Conscription was not imposed and voluntary recruitment, only about 25 per cent of those eligible, was unimpressive. Politically, however, it consolidated the province's position as a strategically vital defensive outpost for the United Kingdom. This earned a grateful loyalty to the unionist cause from a generation of British politicians. Even the Attlee Labour government more or less forgot its historic sympathy with Irish nationalism. On the back of this, the province was able to participate in the Welfare State, allowing the import of Labourism at no political cost to the Unionist united front. In 1949, following the declaration of southern Ireland as a republic, Unionists were gifted the added bonus of the Ireland Act, which for the first time recognized Northern Ireland's right to self-determination.

This new era was slowly to bring its own problems, however. By making Stormont—rather than the people of Northern Ireland consulted through referendum—the final arbiter, control of that assembly became even more crucial and the one-party state was perpetuated. The massive expansion of state largesse, moreover, complicated and brought to the fore Unionist tactics in the manipulation of electoral sectarian geography. The allocation of public housing was not an issue in the interwar period, because hardly any public houses were built. By the 1960s, as slums were cleared and suburbs rose, discriminatory allocation of housing became a major issue. Moreover, state modernization in Great Britain meant that Northern Ireland, simply by standing still, came to look more and more out of step. Already the 1922 Special Powers Act, which allowed for internment, the flogging of prisoners, and other such enormities, looked like a barbaric archaism. From 1949, the property qualification in the local government franchise in Britain was abolished, while it was retained in Northern Ireland. As Britain began tentatively to legislate against racial discrimination in the 1960s, sectarian discrimination in Northern Ireland stood out even more. Unionists added to this sense of differentiation by introducing, in 1954, the Flags and Emblems Act, which effectively illegalized political display of the Irish tricolour in Northern Ireland.

By the late 1950s, as the effects of wartime revitalization of the industrial sector began to fade out, short-term problems presented themselves. There was a marked disaffection of Protestant workers. Even by the mid-1960s, this was beginning to benefit ultra-loyalist opposition to the Ulster Unionist Party, but at first the liberal Northern Ireland Labour Party (NILP) won many Protestant votes. Unionism faced the very real prospect of losing its majority in Belfast. In 1963 Terence O'Neill became Prime Minister with the brief of seeing off the Labour challenge. This he did, with surprising ease, by adopting a technocratic set of policies designed to attract British subventions for renovation of the province's economic superstructure. There was money to spend; but inevitably politicized disputes about how this money would be disbursed. Motorways replaced railways, but the consequence was to downgrade transport links to the west of the province, particularly Derry. A 'new city' was built, but 20 miles from Belfast rather than in an area where consequent population shifts might upset carefully gerrymandered boundaries. Over O'Neill's objections, the Unionist Cabinet gave their model city the provocative name of Craigavon, after the first Prime Minister of Northern Ireland. A second university was built, not in the obvious location of Derry, but in the relatively minor Protestant town of Coleraine. It soon became evident that Derry's Unionist establishment had lobbied behind the scenes, as 'Faceless Men', against Derry's expansion for fear of upsetting the knife-edge gerrymander upon which their control of this majority Catholic city rested. Almost every modernization decision had been twisted against Catholic interests.

Nonetheless, Terence O'Neill sincerely hoped to break the mould of sectarian politics by detaching a section of Catholic opinion from weary Irish nationalism. While O'Neill was no Ulster nationalist—he was much more of the older school of Irish Unionist—he did think that it was possible to draw at least middle-class Catholics into a common Ulster citizenship. O'Neill was the first Northern Ireland Premier to visit Catholic schools, to meet with his southern counterpart, Seán Lemass, and to generally evince a language—not much more than that—of melioration. Of considerable significance for the future, he increased funding for hitherto under-capitalized Catholic schools, the state schools of Northern Ireland having long been secured as Protestant bailiwicks.

O'Neill was almost overthrown in the fraught year of 1966. This was the fiftieth anniversary of the 1916 rebellion, celebrated with great pomp in the south of Ireland. Republicans in the North held their own commemorations, refusing on principle to ask the Northern Ireland authorities for permission to do so. O'Neill nonetheless let them go ahead. On the other hand, when murderous attacks were traced to a small paramilitary loyalist organization, the Ulster Volunteer Force (UVF), O'Neill authorized the use of the Special Powers Act against them, shocking Protestant sensibilities. The Revd Ian Paisley, a young but fiery preacher of the old school, had established his own Free Presbyterian Church, such was his dislike of liberal tendencies in the main denominations. Ever since the Prime Minister's meeting with Seán Lemass in 1964, he had been relentlessly pressing an 'O'Neill Must Go' campaign. Now he organized noisy demonstrations outside the Church of Ireland General Assembly and coat-trailed through the Catholic conclave of Short Strand, sparking a nationalist riot. O'Neill likened Paisleyism to fascism, and Paisley was imprisoned. For most of O'Neill's parliamentary party this was all too much, and they attempted to remove him as Prime Minister. They looked instead to O'Neill's rival within the Cabinet, Minister of Commerce Brian Faulkner. O'Neill survived this move against him by appealing to public opinion in Northern Ireland and in Britain: his defeat, he argued, would be Paisley's victory. As a tactic this was successful. Unionists felt unable to remove him. But O'Neill had effectively defined his own party as a reactionary encumbrance and Paisleyism as the only real alternative to his own brand of liberal unionism.

O'Neill's ambition was to remake unionism in its entirety. Like many others, he thought that the Catholic birth rate meant that they could well become a majority within a generation. It was necessary, he felt, to attract middle-class Catholics into Ulster Unionism, and if the price of this was dropping the obdurate ultra-Protestant wing of the party then so much the better. O'Neill moved with painful slowness, and he would only appeal explicitly for Catholic votes in his last election, held in crisis conditions, in February 1969. Nonetheless, his ambition was to construct a unionism in Northern Ireland that could survive a future Catholic majority, always the Achilles heel of the Northern Ireland partition settlement.

O'Neillism was predicated upon the idea that there was a substantial section of Catholic opinion in the 1960s which wanted no more than 'British rights for British citizens', an illusion of the time which if anything seems to have grown with retrospect. There is precious little evidence for it. To be sure, most Catholics did not believe in Irish unity entirely outside the United Kingdom as anything other than an ultimate ambition. This was not new in the 1960s: the old moderate form of Irish nationalism had survived in Ulster when it died in the rest of Ireland in 1918 precisely because Irish Catholics knew that the reality of Ulster unionism could not be wished away. Nor did this ultimately pragmatic nationalism ever really change. Except, perhaps, for brief moments of maximal passion—around Bloody Sunday in

1972 and possibly the Hunger Strikes in 1981—most Catholics did not believe in or even wish for some kind of nationalist revolution destroying the Union at one fell swoop. The posture of Irish nationalism was much less about an abstract vision of the future and much more about a proud refusal to assimilate into Britishness.

There was a particular nationalist conundrum in the 1960s: the miserable showing of the IRA 'Border Campaign' between 1956 and 1962 seemed evidence of the exhaustion of one nationalist tradition. The general ineptitude, at best avuncular fatalism, of the constitutional Nationalist Party at Stormont only too clearly showed the senility of another. But this was much less a crisis of identity than of political expression. On the plus side of the ledger, the southern Irish economy was performing strongly and, if not yet able to match the living standards of the subsidized North, showed the viability of a successful Irish independence. The gradually accelerating decline of Roman Catholic clerical hegemony also opened the way to a modernization of political expression. This was to take the form, in eminently internationalist style, of a civil rights movement. This had the supreme advantage, even beyond the concrete benefits it might be expected to bring, of undermining Unionist hegemony and underlining that while Northern Ireland, as an entity, might have no foreseeable end-date, it was nonetheless a jerry-built construction of historical impermanence.

The marked modernity of the civil rights movement owes something to the gender balance of Northern Ireland. Unemployment rates were unusually high for men and unusually low for women. The result was still substantial gender inequality favouring men, but less than to be observed in many other Western societies. By 1970, women on average earned 54.9 per cent of men's wages in the Republic of Ireland, and 62 per cent in Northern Ireland. Average annual wages for women in Northern Ireland were 9 per cent higher than for women in Great Britain, whereas for men they were more than 10 per cent lower. Women had a larger share of professional, administrative, and technical posts and a greater proportion of industrial jobs than their counterparts in other regions of the United Kingdom. This was particularly marked in Derry, where the importance of female textile jobs and the high rate of male unemployment meant that women were often breadwinners. As the 1973 Phil Coulter song about the city, 'The Town I Loved So Well', put it:

> In the early morning the shirt factory horn
> Called women from Creggan, the Moor and the Bog
> While the men on the dole played a mother's role
> Fed the children and then trained the dog.

The restoration of masculine pride probably played a significant role in the rapid shift to physical force by 1969, but in the early civil rights movement, women and feminine constructions of community based on local community solidarity undoubtedly played a fructifying role.

The Campaign for Social Justice, established in 1964, was a small middle-class propaganda group led mostly by women. It had the significance of combining a studied eschewal of tired nationalist rhetoric with an often startlingly vehement hostility to the Unionist establishment. Its essentially political goals are revealed by the fact that it paid surprisingly little attention to extremely widespread anti-Catholic discrimination in private employment: it preferred to focus its philippics against Unionist controlled local authorities and Stormont. The Northern Ireland Civil Rights Association (NICRA), formed in 1966 partly on the initiative of the residual IRA, equally avoided overtly nationalist nostrums, but its ambition to maximally embarrass unionism and to delegitimize the Northern Ireland state was never in doubt. With the instinct of the revolutionary, young socialist activists in and around the Labour Party, notably Michael Farrell and

Eamonn McCann, gravitated to the civil rights agitation. In October 1968 they established the People's Democracy as a vehicle.

A protest by the radicals of Derry, the 'capital city of injustice', on 5 October 1968 detonated the mass civil rights movement. The police beat this demonstration off the street but in so doing found they had sown dragon's teeth. Demonstrations proliferated across the North and the Catholic community, more or less regardless of class divisions, united in demands for reform. Terence O'Neill was quick to realize the urgency of the situation and against an unwilling cabinet he drove through a package of reforms in November 1968, though as he himself realized it could not be adequate without the concession of 'one man one vote' (as the sexist language of the time had it) in the local government franchise. This was a bridge too far for unionists, who appreciated that votes weighted by property was the only plausible excuse for gerrymandering. 'One man, one vote' was a talisman for the civil rights movement, which relished the apparent simplicity of such a self-evidently democratic demand.

In some respects we can see the following months as a fuse burning down to Belfast, the real tinderbox where any conflagration would be most ferocious. It is notable that civil rights marchers generally chose country towns in which to march. Indeed, following the November reform package, NICRA agreed to a marching truce and this held until People's Democracy set out on New Year's Day 1969 from Belfast to Derry, in a long march across the North. The marchers were ambushed by loyalists at Burntollet Bridge and again as it entered Derry. That night the RUC ran riot in the Derry Bogside. When civil rights demonstrators themselves rioted in Newry, the following week, the marching truce was effectively reinstated. But now Terence O'Neill, in a failed attempt to win a mandate for his form of liberal unionism, called a general election. It succeeded only in reinforcing the hard-line anti-O'Neill Unionists and demolishing the old Nationalist Party, who were replaced by civil rights leaders.

The fuse burnt frighteningly close to Belfast in April, when loyalist bombs briefly cut off the water supply to the city. O'Neill resigned the premiership, though exacting as a price from his party the concession of 'one man, one vote'.

O'Neill was replaced by James Chichester-Clark, an ineffectual character whose only real advantage was that he was one of the few politicians who was physically taller than Ian Paisley. Chichester-Clark promised the continuation of reform, but it was clear to Catholics that Unionist hearts were not in it. Rather than large-scale demonstrations, however, street clashes with the police and loyalists became the norm as spring turned into summer. All eyes were on the traditional descent of the Protestant 'Apprentice Boys' on Derry in August. Anticipating, perhaps in some ways welcoming, a cathartic confrontation, Catholics in the Bogside of Derry, and to a lesser extent in Belfast, began to prepare material for barricade building. Thousands of milk bottles were purloined to make petrol bombs (Figure 3).

The Apprentice Boys' march in Derry was allowed to take place. Its traditional accompaniment of taunting women—'Orange Lilies'—seemed in particular to aggravate Catholics. Cardinal William Conway issued a complaint: 'I feel bound to say...that I cannot understand why a parade lasting five or six hours and accompanied by dancing women singing Party songs and firing off miniature cannon was allowed to take place in a City which was tinder-dry for an explosion.' Catholic rioting in response turned into an epic three-day struggle with the RUC, a crisis that millions across the British Isles watched on their television screens. Bernadette Devlin of People's Democracy, and now a Westminster MP for Mid-Ulster, was photographed in the thick of it, breaking paving slabs to create missiles and issuing instructions on how to protect against police tear-gas. The burning fuse finally reached Belfast. Catholic areas came under siege from loyalist crowds and panicking police; entire streets were burnt out. If the Bogside looked like a theatrical set-piece battle, almost choreographed and

3. A young rioter during the Battle of the Bogside in August 1969. This iconic image was often reproduced as evidence of an entire community in revolt.

non-lethal, Belfast looked like an incipient civil war. Here seven people were killed. The tattered IRA, mobilized to organize defence, were barely effectual. The Irish government hinted that they might cross the border to protect Catholics—though only in Derry—while the RUC came close to collapse. The B Special police reserve, poorly trained, entirely Protestant, and vehemently unionist, were mobilized, but both Stormont and the British government baulked at the prospect of their being unleashed against Catholics. All options having been exhausted, the British army was deployed on 14 August 'in support of the civil power'.

The British government now felt it had the right to push through radical reform, particularly focused upon the police, which had lost all authority with Catholics. The RUC were disarmed and the B Specials disbanded (to be replaced by the Ulster Defence Regiment under the control of the army). Loyalists were outraged, and rioting broke out on the Protestant Shankill road in Belfast, leading to the death on 11 October 1969 of the first RUC officer in the Troubles. Loyalist fury meant that the Catholic barricades, which had come down after the arrival of troops, began going up again. The authority of the Unionist government could hardly survive this without answer, and it pushed the British government into forcibly deploying the army against these emergent Catholic 'No Go' areas where, behind the barricades, the IRA were beginning to reorganize. As the army repeatedly raided in search of arms, smashing homes as they went, Catholics soon began to see in them their old ineradicably hostile enemy. The IRA had split as 1969 turned into 1970. Both the 'Officials' and the 'Provisionals' turned to armed struggle against the British army, though the Provisionals did so with a determination not much encumbered by political finesse.

In reality, a kind of low-level civil war was under way. Some 15,000 families were forced from their homes in the Greater Belfast area during the period between August 1969 and February 1973. The peaks came in August 1969 and in

August 1971 (when internment was introduced) but the pressure throughout was continuous. Population movements were prompted either by direct physical violence, mostly from Protestant 'loyalists': bricks, petrol-bombs, shootings; specific threats by phone, letter, or graffiti; and 'perceived environmental threats', the miasma of fear that settled across the province. By the time the sorting process had ended, half of Northern Ireland's population lived in areas more than 90 per cent Catholic or Protestant, with only 7 per cent in areas with religious balance roughly 50/50. Divisions were most marked in working-class urban areas. This had the effect, ironically, of lessening the convulsive violence of the earliest years of what now became known as the Troubles. Peace Lines divided battling communities. But Catholic working-class ghettos, expanded by refugees and pummelled by the Army, felt themselves to be simultaneously besieged and occupied. It was the ideal soil for the IRA to sink roots.

In Chapters 2–4, I shall discuss the developing Troubles not as one continuous narrative, but rather from the perspective of the three principal actors: the government (mostly the British government but to an extent the Irish also); the paramilitaries (republican and loyalist); and the 'constitutional parties' (unionist and nationalist).

Chapter 2
The government

The Labour government in London that introduced British troops onto the streets of Northern Ireland was, if anything, ideologically somewhat sympathetic to Irish nationalism. Prime Minister Harold Wilson had been (quite gently) prodding Terence O'Neill to introduce reform since the mid-1960s. Nonetheless, London's priority was stabilizing the situation as soon as possible. James Callaghan, as Home Secretary, saw his role as clearing the unfinished business of civil rights reform while de-escalating the tensions that had exploded in August 1969. His government believed that the relatively moderate leadership of the Unionist government at Stormont was fragile, requiring both cajoling and support. Most importantly, Britain was anxious to sustain the existence of the Stormont system. They feared having to introduce 'direct rule' from London. The logical consequence of this was sustaining the political legitimacy of the Unionist government in Northern Ireland. In effect, this meant the army was defending a political order the legitimacy of which was vanishing for nationalists. British soldiers found themselves battling nationalist rioters. As early as April 1970, responding to serious clashes with Catholics in the Belfast Ballymurphy area, General Freeland warned petrol bombers that they 'would be shot dead in the street'.

The British army

When the Conservatives came to power in the general election of June 1970, the army was turned on the Catholic areas, where the IRA was organizing, with a remit to comb through for arms. This outraged Catholic working-class areas, which feared being exposed to renewed loyalist attack. Army incursions led to regular riots, increasingly orchestrated by republicans. Alienation between Catholics and the army spiralled. Particularly notorious was the curfew imposed on the Falls Road by the fiat of General Freeland between 3 and 5 July 1970. Five civilians were killed and outrage at the curfew 'changed a sullen Catholic Community into a downright hostile one', as Michael Dewar, an army historian, recalled.

The army found itself taking over policing of Catholic areas to an extraordinary extent. The RUC was marginalized because, as Chichester-Clark put it in 1971, 'armed combat is a military task'. This militarization of law and order was inevitably redolent of imperialism. Robin Eveleigh, the 1971 commander of the 3rd Battalion Royal Green Jackets, admitted that 'law enforcement in the republican areas of Northern Ireland was more akin to that in a colony than to that in a self-governing independent state. Ultimately these catholic areas could only be governed by the British by the methods, however mollified, that all occupying nations used to hold down all occupied territories.' The ratchet effect of the first years of the Troubles moved further and further away from anything that looked even vaguely like normal policing. In August 1973 new 'blue card' instructions to soldiers were issued directing them to hand over arrested persons to the Royal Military Police except in 'very exceptional circumstances' when they might be handed over to the RUC.

The army was designed for strong-arm engagement with 'hostiles' which, so far as they were concerned, included the non-paramilitary 'hooligan' youth. A tendency towards brutality was aggravated by a certain military contempt for the Irish. John Hume in October 1971, for example, complained of soldiers singing Orange songs and shouting obscene slogans while on duty in Catholic areas. Nonetheless, it must be said that the army's self-restraint compared well to most civil conflicts and rarely did elements of it run amok. Nonetheless, the encounter of the army with the Catholic crowd, which was more complicatedly gendered than is usually recognized, did much to reinforce nationalist assumptions about British oppression.

On 3 February 1971, searches of houses in the Kashmir Road and Clonard areas of Belfast resulted in an immediate reaction by women and girls who confronted the troops on the streets. They were followed out by the boys and young men of the area. Serious rioting had developed by evening with vehicles set on fire and barricades raised across the Falls Road. The crowds flung petrol and acid bombs, nail bombs, and even grenades. Later that night, machine guns were fired at army posts on the Crumlin Road and Codagon Park on the Malone Road. At a press conference the next day, the Commander-in-Chief of land operations, Major-General Tony Farrar-Hockley, blamed the rioting on the Provisional IRA. He warned of 'a long haul ahead', the first admission by a senior officer that the army might be facing a prolonged campaign. On 6 February the Provisional IRA shot and killed gunner Robert Curtis, the first soldier to die.

Women residents of the New Lodge Road area of Belfast on 11 February paraded outside the army barracks at Birchwood Park, protesting at army behaviour and destruction of property during searches. They demanded a United Nations peacekeeping force to be sent to the district. Ten days later a protest march from Old Park to Ardoyne was led by six women dressed in combat jackets (the wearing of military-style uniforms indicating membership of subversive organzations was banned shortly afterwards). The Shankill Road Loyalist Women's Action Committee organized a counter-picket: 'If security forces don't take action against uniformed women the Women of the Shankill will.' Thirty women and six men, all republicans, were duly arrested. Rioting again erupted, this time sweeping in particular the Catholic Markets area, a city centre enclave close to Belfast Magistrates Court.

IRA attacks on the army proliferated. Brian Faulkner, the Prime Minister at Stormont, on 26 May announced: 'At this moment any soldier seeing a person with a weapon or acting suspiciously may fire to warn or with effect depending on circumstances without waiting for orders.' This was dangerous, as 'firing to warn' was a very low threshold. The British government did not demur, however, and the Conservative Home Secretary, Reginald Maudling, told a private meeting on 28 July 1971 that a state of war now existed between the IRA and the British army. To a large extent, of course, this was forced by the IRA onto the British government. But there was also an element of choice about it. The British consciously chose to turn their firepower on the more 'acceptable' enemy. As Maudling admitted, 'we had to remember all the time that the Protestants could be just as violent as the Catholics, and they were far more numerous. . . . A Protestant backlash was the great danger we all feared.'

Unionists pushed hard for the introduction of internment (imprisonment without trial). The army was not enthusiastic, General Tuzo repeatedly pointing out that they lacked sufficient intelligence on who to lift. Arresting only nationalists, he feared, would simply unite the Catholic community against the security forces. His pessimistic prognosis was amply proven. The introduction of internment on 9 August 1971, Operation Demetrius, was designed to crack the organizational capability of the IRA, targeting nationalist males of military age (no females were interned until January 1973). On the first morning, 337 were arrested, though a quarter of those targeted escaped the drag-net. It did nothing to still disorder; quite the contrary. Within three days, twenty-three people had been killed in the massive upsurge of rioting and gun battles. News of the use of torture on internees soon leaked out: in most cases straightforward assault and battery, but for selected victims, refined techniques based upon hunger-rations, hooding, stress-posture, deafening 'white noise', and sleep deprivation. Brutal live fire against rioters in anti-internment riots (notably the notorious Ballymurphy massacre of 9/10 August 1971, in which twelve civilians were killed) further damaged the reputation of the army (Figure 4).

Soldiers were still bound by Yellow Card rules of engagement, which meant that, contrary to Faulkner's assertion, live firing was only authorized in the face of immediate risk to life. Rounds could only be fired when use of lethal force against those targeted was legally justified. This meant that soldiers were forbidden to use firing either to intimidate or to injure. The army's automatic

4. A painting of a border road in County Fermanagh being 'cratered' with explosives by the British army in the early 1970s (the painter, Christopher Miers, was himself a soldier). The intention was to prevent the IRA moving across from relative safety in the south of Ireland. The Brexit controversy raised fears that the border could again become a flashpoint.

weapons were set to fire single shots on each trigger pull. As a consequence, free-fire, with its inevitable attendant casualties, never became the norm. Army heroes, too, need to be acknowledged. On 25 May 1971, a gelignite bomb was thrown into the reception area of the joint army–RUC command post on the Springfield Road in Belfast. Sergeant Willetts, of the 3rd Parachute Regiment, was killed when he stepped between the blast and children who were inside the building at the time.

The Bloody Sunday massacre of January 1972 showed homicidal army force at its worst. The Parachute Regiment killed thirteen unarmed civilians. John Peck, the British ambassador in Dublin and a veteran of decolonization, was shaken by 'a wave of fury and exasperation the like of which I had never encountered in my life, in Egypt or Cyprus or anywhere else. Hatred of the British was intense.' At Westminster, Bernadette Devlin, MP for Mid-Ulster, crossed the floor to Reginald Maudling's seat and slapped him. Maudling is reported to have said, with patronizing hauteur, that he was used to having his hair pulled by his grandchildren.

Direct rule

London's responsibility notwithstanding, the massacre finally triggered the proroguing of Stormont on 30 March. The British government imposed direct rule. Unionists were understandably annoyed that they were paying the price for a British mistake. William Whitelaw, who was appointed as the first Secretary of State to Northern Ireland, to act as a kind of viceroy, was less than sympathetic about their complaints when he found what Unionist rule had really meant. In his diaries Cecil King recorded Whitelaw's complaint that 'the Augean stables were nothing to the mess he found at Stormont, disproportionate ministerial salaries for Ministers; jobs for the Protestant boys; every power of the government used to depress the Catholics. Whitelaw obviously thought that the Catholics had far more to put up with than he had realized.' British political opinion was in a mood to deliver something to Irish nationalism.

Having disavowed any radical political initiative for two years, Britain now swung the other way. In June 1972 they opened up talks with the Provisional IRA and a ceasefire for talks was agreed. The time seemed propitious. The IRA had won a major victory with the bringing down of Stormont and could call off its armed struggle with dignity. Almost all prisoners were internees, convicted of no crime and detained in obviously temporary camps, and could quite easily be released in the event of an overall settlement. The relatively small number of convicted prisoners no doubt would follow suit. The Official IRA had already called a ceasefire at the end of March (and its interned prisoners were soon let out).

Nonetheless, the talks with the Provisional IRA held on 7 July 1972 in London did not get very far. It is difficult to be certain how far they might have gone: William Whitelaw angered his interlocutors by boasting, ridiculously, that the British army would never fire on unarmed civilians. More importantly, the British side was not impressed by the tone of demand from the IRA representatives at the talks. Whitelaw did however promise that the Cabinet would 'carefully consider' an all-Ireland referendum on the border, the IRA's key demand, and a further meeting was scheduled for a week's time. British officials later discussing the meeting wondered 'whether the position of the IRA leaders was to be regarded as an opening bid which was negotiable'. They noted that the Declaration of Intent raised as a demand by the IRA was 'very close to the position of Mr Lynch [Taoiseach of Ireland] that the future of Ireland should be decided by the people of Ireland as a whole'.

Loyalist pressure and British army heavy-handedness, however, gave the hardliners in the Provisional IRA an opportunity to scupper the talks. British troops on duty at Lenadoon Avenue, watched approvingly by the loyalist paramilitary Ulster Defence Association, fired rubber bullets and CS gas at a hostile Catholic crowd. The commander of the Provisional IRA Belfast Brigade, Seamus Twomey, told the army commander that he considered the British army to have violated the truce. Some hours later, a formal announcement from the Provisional IRA in Dublin declared that the ceasefire had ended and that all IRA units had been instructed to resume offensive action. Nine people were killed in the fighting that spread throughout Belfast over the weekend, including one army free-fire incident at Springhill where a priest, Father Fitzpatrick, one youth member of the IRA, and three civilians, all of them unarmed, were killed.

Whitelaw, humiliated by the entire affair, hurried to disavow talks with the IRA. The British government, he said, was committed to a political reconciliation of the communities 'whether the extremists on either side like it or not', and if the IRA returned to its campaign with ferocity, 'we will retaliate with the same ferocity'. Nonetheless, this abortive attempt to bring in the extremes proved damaging for British policy in the long run. Given the ingrained suspicion of British intentions in Northern Ireland, a hundred statements asserting the government's determination not to give in to the men of violence could not compensate for one secretive negotiation with the IRA. Unionist suspicion of British bona fides remained acute and republican expectations that eventually Britain must sit down and seriously engage with their demands remained high.

Britain attempted to repair the damage by explicitly excluding the IRA from the political process it now launched. This meant that it was not prepared to countenance anything which suggested a let-up of security force pressure against the IRA. The next two years, therefore, saw an attempt to build a settlement, based upon drawing together the unionist and nationalist middle ground, in the midst of a low-level war. It is not surprising, therefore, that it failed.

On 31 July 1972, following escalating pressure from loyalist barricade builders, the British army launched 'Operation Motorman', the removal of barricades surrounding republican controlled areas in Derry and Belfast. The IRA preferred to lie low rather than to stand and fight, and no resistance was offered (though the army killed two civilians). In Claudy village, twelve miles from Derry, three IRA car bombs exploded killing nine civilians. The Londonderry coroner, who had earlier condemned British actions on Bloody Sunday as 'sheer, unadulterated murder', called the Claudy attack 'sheer, unadulterated, cold, calculating, fiendish murder'. The IRA had taken an enormous public relations and operational hit, and the almost 5,500 shooting incidents in the four months up to Motorman nearly halved in the four months following. As William Whitelaw recalled, 'we had succeeded beyond our wildest dreams'. The way was clear for a political initiative.

A government Green Paper ('The Future of Northern Ireland') issued in October 1972 summarized the positions of the main parties but the most significant contribution was London's tentative acceptance of an 'Irish dimension' in any settlement. John Hume of the SDLP said it contained 'the first glimmerings of reality that Northern problems should be faced in an Irish context'. A subsequent White Paper proposed an elected Northern Ireland Assembly and a devolved government based on some form of power-sharing between the political parties, both unionist and nationalist. The Secretary of State, however, would continue in office, and control of security matters would remain with Westminster. The 'Irish dimension' was catered for by a proposal to set up a Council of Ireland for North–South discussion on relevant matters. The White Paper reaffirmed that Northern Ireland would remain part of the United Kingdom for as long as that was the wish of the majority of the people there. Harold Wilson for the Labour Opposition unhelpfully warned that if Ulster rejected the principles of the White Paper it must inevitably 'mean an agonising reappraisal of the Great Britain–Northern Ireland relationship'.

Elections to the Assembly took place in June 1973, with a 72 per cent turnout. The largest single bloc of Unionists elected was anti-White Paper, but the Unionists led by Brian Faulkner were prepared to negotiate with Britain and opposition parties. On 21 November, agreement was reached between the parties to establish a power-sharing government, with ministerial portfolios distributed between unionists, nationalists, and those in between. Devolution was restored and only the Council of Ireland issue was outstanding. On 6 December 1973, Prime Minister Edward Heath welcomed the power-sharing parties from Northern Ireland and the Irish government to tripartite talks at Sunningdale in Berkshire. After three days of tortuous talks, agreement was reached. The Irish government acknowledged that there could be no unity without the consent of the majority in Northern Ireland; Britain promised not to stand in the way of unification if that consent was forthcoming; and the structure and scope of a Council of Ireland with executive powers was set out. Any powers given to the Council would have to be agreed by the Northern Ireland Assembly, but there was no reverse gear. It looked to many unionists like a one-way ratchet in the direction of a United Ireland. Nationalists were not entirely happy either, however: there was little reform offered to soften the security regime.

The Sunningdale Agreement was based upon an algebraic formula that Britain was to consistently adhere to for the rest of the Troubles, at least in theory. This involved three elements. First was an internal settlement, based upon the restoration of devolution, and compulsory power-sharing between nationalists and unionists. Second was an East–West settlement, in which the two sovereign governments of the United Kingdom and Ireland would agree a common line on politics in the province, while sovereignty remained with Britain. Third was a North–South settlement, in which some kind of cross-border institutions would be constructed. The problem with this was that the East–West and North–South institutions could be as restrictive or expansive as pressure from the actors in Northern Ireland might make them.

This, in some respects, was the worst of both worlds. It annoyed nationalists who felt that it did not go far enough in undermining partition, and it terrified unionists who saw it as opening the road to a united Ireland.

The power-sharing government in Northern Ireland was dealt a nearly fatal blow by an exterior shock. British contingencies, particularly a miners' strike, drove Edward Heath into calling a UK-wide general election for 28 February 1974. Michael McKeown, a moderate nationalist, was horrified:

> I was driving home over the Queen's Bridge in Belfast and turned on the 4 o'clock news on the car radio. I was dismayed to hear that he had decided to go to the country. I found it nearly incredible. I was...staggered that, as the British Prime Minister who had come close to a settlement of the Irish problem, he should put that settlement in jeopardy because of his emotional involvement in the miners' dispute....The woman on the Shankill was right: 'You can never trust the frigging British.'

The anti-agreement unionists used this election as a referendum on Sunningdale. In this, they were successful, increasing their share of the vote from 35.4 per cent at the time of the Assembly election in June 1973 to 51.2 per cent, a swing of 15.8 per cent unprecedented in British politics. The pro-Sunningdale parties could only cling on and hope that they would have recovered in time for the next assembly elections due in four years.

The IRA, though somewhat contained by the army, nonetheless kept up maximum pressure, and bombings were frequent. Loyalists, for their part, called a general strike in opposition to the agreement on 15 May. After a slow start, it soon became crippling. Half-hearted attempts were made to bring over specialist soldiers to keep vital services running, but it was an impossible task. The Ministry of Defence in London, deeply unenthusiastic and suspicious of Harold Wilson's newly elected Labour government, dragged its feet. Wilson made a television broadcast that roundly abused the strikers but pointedly did not even mention the main issue of contention—the Council of Ireland. In practice, his strong language masked a willingness to capitulate. The Ulster Workers Council (UWC), organizing the strike, saw this clearly.

Britain's refusal to talk to the UWC placed all the pressure on the power-sharing executive, as it was meant to do. Petrol supplies were running low, and when the army took over a few petrol stations it was too late. The pro-Sunningdale Unionists led by Faulkner gave up the ghost on 28 May. Their abandonment of the power-sharing executive collapsed the whole scheme. Britain's attempts to build on the middle ground had fallen apart.

Edward Heath, now out of power, was furious with his successors. The power-sharing executive, he pointed out, had 'worked efficiently and well' until the 'Labour Government under Mr Wilson failed to give it the support it required from H.M. forces to break the petrol lorry drivers strike in May 1974. The lesson to be learnt from that episode is that without such support, either from its own resources or from the United Kingdom Government, no administration in Northern Ireland will ever survive.' According to an SDLP Minister at the time, Austin Currie, the army 'were unwilling to take action when they could not be sure of the end result.... The GOC [Sir Frank King, commanding the army in Northern Ireland] feared...a confrontation with the UWC and...a war on two fronts.' There seems to be something to this. On 3 September 1974, in the right wing Monday Club magazine *Monday World*, an army officer, under the pseudonym Andrew Sefton, commented that the 'unwillingness' of the army to end the UWC strike and the 'subsequent confrontation between the military and the politicians, must be the most significant event of recent years'. Years later, General King confirmed that the army had indeed intended to refuse any order to move against loyalist barricades.

Merlyn Rees, the new Labour Secretary of State, was convinced that the strike represented the upsurge of the entire Protestant community against British sovereign right. In his memoir of the period, he argued that 'Ulster loyalists were loyal to a Protestant Northern Ireland, not to the United Kingdom.... It went along with something I began to call Ulster Nationalism.' A memorandum he produced for Harold Wilson immediately following the UWC strike, on 31 May, advised him to 'Let the Ulstermen try to work it out between themselves' in the hope that 'a new Ulster identity to include the republicans' would coalesce. A paper produced by civil servants early in June to discuss 'options', however, warned that unilateral British withdrawal would lead to major violence: 'Dominion status' or near independence for Northern Ireland, it concluded, was a 'pipe-dream'. As Rees concluded, 'My only hope for the future was that the "Ulster nationalism" of the loyalists would grow into something capable of uniting a divided community.'

Britain laboured under the illusion that Unionism was a kind of embryonic Ulster nationalism, and that the Protestants of Northern Ireland valued Stormont as a fundamental expression of their identity. If this was the case, then one might expect unionists to agree to power-sharing and an Irish dimension in order to get their Stormont back. They might even be willing to weaken or even let loose the connection with Britain. In reality, however, unionists had been attached to Stormont primarily as a block on any move to a united Ireland by the British government. By the mid-1970s, it seemed clear to them that direct rule, including a unionist veto on constitutional innovation, was the most secure bulwark of the Union. They had no incentive to make any substantive concessions for a return to Stormont.

Briefly, the Labour government turned again to an attempt to 'bring in the extremes', hoping that a political disintegration of the unionist and nationalist middle ground would tempt the paramilitaries to move into the vacuum and away from their paramilitary campaigns. Even before Sunningdale collapsed, both Sinn Féin (banned in Northern Ireland since 1956) and the Ulster Volunteer Force were legalized (the Ulster Defence Association had never been proscribed). Merlyn Rees's announcement to the House of Commons in June 1974 that Britain would not 'pull out quickly' from Northern Ireland was not exactly reassuring for unionists.

The British negotiated a truce with the Provisional IRA, who were feeling optimistic that Britain was seeking a way out of the imbroglio, and this took effect on 9 February 1975. 'Incident centres' were established in various parts of Northern Ireland staffed by civil servants on a twenty-four-hour basis to act as points of contact in either direction, and as a preliminary stage to further discussions. Seamus Lachlan, Provisional Sinn Féin organizer for Belfast, announced that IRA patrols would patrol in republican areas. Behind the scenes British representatives secretly reassured the IRA that Britain had no stomach for staying in Northern Ireland and that they were looking for a politically acceptable way out. The Dublin government was horrified, and made known its deep concern that the elected representatives of the Roman Catholic community were being bypassed.

Very quickly, however, it became apparent that the politically obdurate centre ground was consolidating rather than collapsing. Elections to a new Constitutional Convention were announced in March 1975. An attempt by the UDA and the UVF to strong-arm the unionist leadership and force adoption of their candidates was rebuffed. After considerable prevarication, Sinn Féin declared in April, three days before nominations closed, that they would boycott the forthcoming Convention elections. It did not help that British representatives covertly hinted to the IRA that they would move towards withdrawal if the Convention failed. The results of the election substantially reproduced the post-Sunningdale political deadlock. 'It is the same old faces with the same old arguments,' an Ulster housewife told a reporter. 'It never worked before so why should it work now?'

With nothing new on the political horizon, therefore, there was little coherent in the British negotiating strategy. As a senior British civil servant, Sir Frank Cooper, put it, the government's reasoning was that 'we did not think [the Provisional] IRA were beaten' and so the intention was to 'string them along' in the hope that their capacity for violence would fade away. Instead, IRA violence redirected away from the security forces towards republican rivals, loyalists, and Protestant civilians. The year 1976 was probably the lowest point of the Troubles: not in terms of absolute violence—1972 has that grim laurel—but in terms of sheer, demoralizing brutality (Figure 5). So far as Rees was concerned, violence had simply become an Ulster disease, 'a traditional way of life for them in some parts of the North'.

5. While a farmer and part-time member of the Ulster Defence Regiment, a locally recruited unit of the British army, goes about his work, his wife stands in defence against IRA assassination attempts. Particularly in rural areas Protestant families often felt besieged by the republican threat.

In September 1975, the IRA announced that it would 'retaliate' against violations of the Truce by security forces, and in November Britain closed its incident centres, saying they no longer played any useful role. Technically the Truce dragged on into 1976, but in reality it had fizzled out long before.

Deadlock

The British government had never concretely offered the IRA more than slow surrender. It showed no willingness to confront the unionist veto on constitutional change which had been demonstrated so dramatically when Sunningdale had been brought down. Britain quickly readjusted its posture so that it was simply orchestrating a containment of the Northern Ireland problem. This amounted to treating violence as a criminal rather than a political problem, and beefing up the RUC, which had been almost entirely marginalized by the British army. In March 1976, Rees announced the restoration of police 'primacy' in security policy. This strategy of 'Ulsterization' was confirmed in a White Paper issued in March 1977, though at the same time it was publicized that SAS Special Forces had been deployed against the IRA in South Armagh. This was an area, overwhelmingly republican in sympathy, where the army knew themselves to be in essence an occupying force. 'It was very lonely out there,' a soldier wrote of his tour in 1976, 'the whole atmosphere is charged with hatred and I can feel eyes watching us from behind curtained windows and hedgerows. We are right in the heart of their country and they only have to bide their time before zapping us again.' The island of Great Britain, it was hoped, could be protected from such 'zapping' by the Prevention of Terrorism Act, a measure passed in 1974 which concentrated on quarantining Northern Ireland from Great Britain. By 1981, more than 5,000 had been arrested under the Act, mostly at ports and airports, though only about 300 were charged with any criminal offence. Almost 250 exclusion orders were placed on people from all parts of Ireland forbidding their entry into Great Britain.

To a large extent police 'primacy' was something of a myth. The army continued at the cutting edge of insurgency. What really marked the security forces was a kind of 'masculine primacy' which extended across the security forces. Many young working-class soldiers enjoyed the buzz of power and confrontation, a step-up from civilian aggro on the streets of Britain. 'It would be just a punch here, a kick there, the odd head-butt or dig in the ribs with a rifle,' remembered one soldier of his interaction with Irish locals. 'And, so far as I was concerned, I never hit anyone who didn't ask for it.' Even as the RUC was effectively militarized, female officers were forbidden to carry arms and women were dismissed from the police reserve. In March 1987, thirty-one RUC women won a sex discrimination case against the Chief Constable Sir John Hermon and were awarded £240,000 compensation. Sir John agreed to end discriminatory practices and offered women equal access to all training and employment opportunities. This was one of the less unifying examples of female advancement in Northern Ireland.

The new Secretary of State, Roy Mason, when appointed towards the end of 1976, made clear his disdain for any bright schemes of political innovation. 'I thought it futile to barge in with great plans and programs and proposals for constitutional change,' he wrote. 'The terrorists just weren't interested in listening. Their interest was in killing and destroying....All our resources have to be focused against them.' Political innovation, it seemed, had simply frightened unionists and encouraged the republicans. Britain now hoped that if it stopped stirring the pot, violence in Northern Ireland would simmer down and in due course disappear.

The Conservative Party while in opposition came very close to rejecting even power-sharing as a dead end. Only after the election of Margaret Thatcher in 1979 did they retreat from this position, under pressure from the Irish government which made clear that it would internationally condemn Britain if it reneged on even the prospect of constitutional reform in Northern Ireland.

Nonetheless, Britain's commitment to actively securing a settlement was hardly more than verbal by the end of the 1970s and into the early 1980s.

James Prior, appointed as Secretary of State for Northern Ireland in September 1981, knew well that he was being politically sidelined as a sceptic of hard-line Thatcherism. He later complained that the Northern Ireland Office was regarded by British politicians as a dustbin. He found his new job anomalous.

> As the Secretary of State for Northern Ireland I found myself performing a dual role, as a Governor-General representing the Queen and as such the enemy of every republican in the Province, but also as a Secretary of State acting like a referee in the boxing ring whose authority seemed to be resented equally by both sides....My political role was unique in itself. I was the head of Government, yet my own political base was not in the Province but across of the Irish Sea in Britain. On many occasions I felt as though I was a foreigner in another land.

Britain, essentially, still felt that it was unwillingly occupying a part of a hostile country.

With little support from London, Prior initiated the 'Rolling Devolution' scheme, in which an Assembly elected in Northern Ireland would be empowered to take over bit by bit any governmental functions the political parties could agree to share power on. This was never likely to get anywhere. The SDLP pointed out that the unionist leadership would only agree to those few elements of power-sharing it would be comfortable with, and would not even consider an Irish dimension. James Molyneaux of the Ulster Unionists accurately enough described the Assembly as nothing more than a 'devolved talking-shop'. The government invested no political capital in this scheme. Thatcher's frame of analysis suggested little more than managing the natives with minimum fuss. 'We are dealing with fear, suspicion and folklore,' she told the Irish Taoiseach (Prime Minister), 'not a problem that would be resolved simply by reason and common sense. The problem was to find a way through the difficulties in a manner and at a rate that would not cause it to blow up in our faces.'

British attempts at depoliticized 'normalization' led directly to the prisons controversy and the 1981 hunger strikes. The republican movement was determined to resist their treatment as nothing other than criminals or 'godfathers of crime'. The election on 9 April 1981 of Bobby Sands, the first hunger striker, to the Westminster seat of Fermanagh and South Tyrone was deeply embarrassing for Britain. A Representation of the People Act was rushed through to ban prisoners standing for Parliament. Nonetheless, a republican candidate, Owen Carron, won the seat (on an abstentionist ticket) following Sands's death.

This was immediately damaging for Britain, from a propaganda point of view. It undermined the idea that the 'men of violence' were simply criminals. More importantly, it showed that even if Britain was not actively 'stirring the pot' with controversial political initiatives, its very attempt to 'normalize' the situation could create a blowback in terms of Catholic–nationalist alienation and escalating IRA violence. The hunger strikes fundamentally undermined the entire premise of British government policy since 1975. The situation was made worse by the subsequent rise of Sinn Féin as a considerable electoral force. By 1983, they were a serious challenge to the SDLP.

The Anglo-Irish Agreement

Since the end of 1980 there had been an Anglo-Irish political process to discuss 'possible new institutional structures, citizenship rights, security matters, economic co-operation and measures to encourage mutual understanding'. At first this had been simply a means of keeping the Irish government on side and it was often strained. In the aftermath of the hunger strikes, however, the Irish began to get a real hearing. In particular, they pointed out the problem of Catholic 'alienation' from the institutions of government in Northern Ireland. It was this, they argued, that sustained the IRA campaign and which could at any point erupt into a real crisis of popular insurgency. As the New Ireland Forum of nationalist parties, excluding Sinn Féin, reported in 1984, 'There are at present no political institutions to which a majority of people of the nationalist and unionist traditions can give their common allegiance or even acquiesce in.' The Irish argued that this alienation could only be overcome by reforming the governance of Northern Ireland so that the Irish identity of nationalists in Northern Ireland could be acknowledged, recognized, and even legitimized. Irish nationalists in Northern Ireland could not be expected to identify with purely British rule no matter how 'normalizing' its philosophy of governance might be.

This was the Irish line in the political negotiations that led to a 1985 Anglo-Irish Agreement. Margaret Thatcher had little natural sympathy for anything outside the British constitutional modulation. Her colleagues in Cabinet and even more so the British civil service (the civil service of Northern Ireland was kept out of the loop) were more than half convinced by the Irish analysis, however. They were able to play upon Thatcher's instinct for activism and to chivvy her into the most radical governmental initiative since Sunningdale.

The Anglo-Irish Agreement was remarkable in that it effectively conceded that the British government could not hope to win the dutiful allegiance of Catholics in Northern Ireland by its own right. While British sovereignty remained, the Irish government was given an automatic right of consultation on any policy which related in any way to the interests of nationalists in Northern Ireland; this effectively covered the entire ambit of governance in Northern Ireland.

The agreement was not meant to be a comprehensive settlement in itself but it did open up the possibility of one. Direct rule had been entirely comfortable for unionists. The agreement, however, meant that direct rule came at the price of Irish interference in Northern Ireland. Unionists could only unpick this by agreeing to devolution, which would remove swathes of governance from the responsibility of the Secretary of State and so also from the Irish government's automatic right of consultation. The price of devolution, of course, would be power-sharing and some kind of Irish dimension.

Thatcher, who had never been particularly comfortable with the agreement, was quickly disillusioned when IRA violence continued unabated. She turned to one last attempt to break the IRA by main force, introducing in 1988 a raft of legislation, restricting the traditional 'right to remain silent' for those arrested and introducing censorship of apologists for political violence on broadcast media. The British army was given licence to adopt a much harder line against the IRA. Though Yellow Card rules were not formally lifted, the army felt encouraged to contrive situations where they could intercept IRA Active Service Units in the field and annihilate them. The ambush at Loughgall in 1987, when a joint army–RUC operation cornered and killed eight IRA men, plus an unfortunate civilian passer-by, was the most striking example. Not all such operations were successful.

The peace process

Behind the scenes, however, the British government were beginning to reach out to the IRA, and secret negotiations began in 1989. These were accelerated after the replacement of Margaret Thatcher by John Major as Conservative leader and Prime Minister in November 1990. Having faced down unionist opposition to the Anglo-Irish Agreement the British government were able to cajole the unionists at last into serious political negotiations with nationalists.

In the 1970s, negotiations had been at a forced pace. The Troubles then had been an intense crisis of a few years. A sense of urgency and immediacy had hung over this 'first peace process'. Britain, however, had concluded that this very sense of urgency and immediacy simply aggravated unionist fears and encouraged republican hopes, making the situation worse rather than better. Now the approach taken was one of deliberate slowness. The political process was drawn out through almost the entirety of the 1990s. While Sunningdale had been an attempt to find a political settlement without directly addressing the problem of political violence, this time a distinct if connected 'peace process' accompanied the political process. This was similarly step by step. The IRA called a ceasefire in 1994, broke it off, but restored it in 1997.

Britain set the broad parameters—devolution, power-sharing, and Irish dimension—but allowed the practicalities to emerge from the political actors in Northern Ireland. When the New Labour government came into power in 1997, Tony Blair and his colleagues committed an extraordinary focus of attention on Northern Ireland. This was partly because, for electoral purposes, they had signed up to the broad outlines of Conservative spending plans, so there was relatively little domestic innovation the government could attempt in its first term. The rather bland millenarianism of the 1990s Third Way, moreover, was unexpectedly helpful. Alastair Campbell, Blair's press adviser, recorded an exchange shortly after Labour's election in May 1997. 'TB said he reckoned he could see a way of sorting the Northern Ireland problem. I loved the way he said it, like nobody had thought of it before.' It seemed that historical problems once thought intractable could be resolved by elegant triangulation.

For this problem and at this particular juncture, triangulation was indeed productive. It allowed for settlement by bricolage, with each Northern Ireland interest group being allowed something they could sell to their constituency. This meant demilitarization and prisoner release for republicans and loyalists, the abrogation of the Anglo-Irish Agreement for the unionists, and power-sharing for the SDLP. There was an IRA commitment to 'exclusively peaceful means' as a fundamental minimum for unionism and referendums held concurrently on both sides of the border, to represent all Ireland self-determination, as a minimum for nationalism. The Belfast Agreement of 1998, signed on 10 April, Good Friday, was not supported by the DUP, but nonetheless was successfully ratified by dual referendums. A new and more hopeful era in Northern Ireland had begun.

Chapter 3
Paramilitarism

In the early 20th century Ireland had been a pioneer in the culture of paramilitarism. The establishment of the loyalist Ulster Volunteer Force in 1912, the Labour-socialist Irish Citizens Army in 1913, the nationalist Irish Volunteers, and the republican-feminist Cumann na mBan in 1914 were precursors to widespread paramilitarism across Europe, usually ultra-nationalist or radically left wing, in the interwar period. The catastrophe of fascism and the peril of communism more or less expunged the continental culture of paramilitarism in the period after 1945. But in Ireland, the tradition never met with the same kind of moral wreck. The Ulster Volunteer Force became a founding myth for Northern Ireland and the annual Orange parades of drum-and-fife bands, a quasi-formal institution of the state, certainly did much to keep uniforms and marching feet a central part of public imagination. After the 1916 Rebellion the Irish Volunteers evolved into the Irish Republican Army (IRA) which waged a war of independence against Britain between 1919 and 1921. Though active IRA Volunteers were a small minority very many more people found themselves in defiance of British law. The romantic glamour of patriotic defiance was an important and enduring driver for militancy. One English feminist, Evelyn Sharp, sympathized with an Irish woman whose fiancé was on the run. 'And do you think I'd be engaged to a man who was *not* on the run?' she responded proudly. The sexual allure of heroic action would not be the least of paramilitary recruiting sergeants during the Troubles.

In the 1921 Treaty negotiations between Britain and republican Ireland, the British side insisted upon denying independent Ireland its desire for status as a republic. Partly this was due to a sentimental attachment to the mythos of the Crown but Britain was also anxious to deny the IRA a moral victory to add to its political and propaganda-war victory, for fear of radicalizing anticolonial opinion in the empire. The result was an IRA which had 'won the war' but felt little or no ownership of the 'Free State', the new independent Irish administration backed by Britain as an alternative to the republic.

In 1922 civil war broke out between the Free State and IRA irreconcilables. The IRA was defeated by 1923, but it did not simply disappear. Rather, it took comfort in its ideological purity and went underground. By the 1960s, the IRA was a pale shadow of its former self but its reputation as nation-builders and redoubtable, unconquerable rebels remained potent. Entirely on its own initiative, it was able to launch an armed campaign against partition in 1956, which dragged on in desultory fashion until 1962. As its ceasefire statement made clear, the campaign had failed miserably due to lack of support from the people. Nonetheless, it was evident that an armed cadre with ample reserves of sympathy, if not active support, was both self-sustaining and steeped in organizational experience.

Resurgence

It was loyalism which made the first move in what is generally considered to be the modern 'Troubles' in Northern Ireland. In 1966 a small group in Belfast resurrected the name of the Volunteer Force (UVF) to carry out a series of sectarian attacks on Catholics, culminating in murder. Though the stated target was members of the IRA, in reality this was an offensive undertaken with the intention of undermining the reformist unionism of Terence O'Neill. This was to become characteristic of loyalism, which reacted more to the perceived establishment sell-out of the Union than it did directly to IRA predations.

After the failure of the Border Campaign, the IRA turned sharply to the left and adopted a version of the communist 'popular front' strategy: the establishment of front organizations that could mobilize and radicalize a sympathetic constituency which the disciplined cadre could then recruit from. To this end, republicans were prime movers in the establishment, in 1966, of the Northern Ireland Civil Rights Association. It would be wrong to say that republicans controlled this organization in any straightforward sense. This was especially the case when a civil rights mass movement emerged in October 1968. Indeed, the real radicals of the civil rights period were the revolutionary-socialist left, broadly in the Trotskyist tradition, rather than the republicans, who were anxious not to put at risk the pan-class solidarity of Irish nationalism. The government appointed 'Cameron Commission' in its 1969 Report was positively commending of IRA restraint in civil rights activism.

Loyalism was energized by the threat it saw in the civil rights movement. Its aim was not so much to defeat republicanism as to draw it out into the open as much as possible, to prevent it 'hiding' behind the civil rights movement, and to force the Unionist government to use coercion against it. Loyalism always saw itself as a force multiplier for the armed resources of the state. In the first months of the civil rights movement, this meant loyalist counter-protests, generally led by Ian Paisley, which would block any civil rights march from moving out from a residential area defined as nationalist into the common public space of city or town centres. This had the effect of publicly stamping the civil rights movement as being essentially nationalist and subversive rather than, as it claimed to be, neutral on the border question and reformist. It was an effective strategy because, to a great extent, civil rights leaders were indeed of a nationalist bent. They did desire to delegitimize the Northern Ireland government and by extension both Stormont and partition, and the marches did put on the streets large numbers of people who were certainly committed to traditional aspirations for a United Ireland. IRA Volunteers often served as (rather effective and moderating) stewards for civil rights marches. Loyalist counter-protests forced the Royal Ulster Constabulary (RUC) to stop civil rights marchers from walking the agreed route for fear of public disorder arising from collision with the Paisleyites. This was, in the loyalist view, simply obliging the RUC to carry out its fundamental duty to suppress nationalist subversion. Certainly, the ordinary members of the RUC, 80 per cent Protestant and, so far as we can tell, almost entirely unionist, were more or less willing participants in this political-policing script.

A key point in the evolution of Northern Ireland paramilitarism was the Stormont general election called by Terence O'Neill in February 1969. This was because of something which did not happen, rather than something that did happen. Northern Ireland had drifted so far into the crisis that the old political establishment parties were in the process of disintegration, but not so far that the politics represented by the paramilitaries could take advantage. Sinn Féin, which was still illegal, did not stand in the 1969 elections even under a front name (though they did support the successful by-election candidature of the young left-wing socialist Bernadette Devlin in the Westminster constituency of Mid-Ulster in the following month). This meant that the disintegration of the long-standing Nationalist Party worked to the advantage of electorally minded, middle-class, and reformist nationalists who would later go on to form the Social Democratic and Labour Party (SDLP). Working-class loyalism, meanwhile, flowed to the Paisleyite Protestant Unionist Party and sundry anti-O'Neill Unionists that would become the seedbed for the evangelical and petty-bourgeois Democratic Unionist Party (DUP).

This set up a context which for republicans, in particular, was in sharp contrast to their glory days in the early 20th century. Then Sinn Féin had established itself as the voice of the people before its armed wing, the IRA, initiated serious armed actions against the British government. When it came to negotiations in 1921, Britain had politically mandated interlocutors to talk with. The problem the IRA had in the first phase of the Northern Ireland Troubles was that they had no strong political wing with an electoral mandate. After February 1969 there was to be no other Stormont general election until it was shut down by Britain in March 1972. Thereafter, successive elections were held to weigh the support of political parties invited in advance to negotiations by the British government, political processes that explicitly excluded republicans. The outcome was that the peak of IRA 'armed struggle' in 1972 was completely out of sync with its electoral breakthrough nearly a decade later. This would make it almost impossible for the IRA to convert its violent 'propaganda of the deed' into a strong negotiating position in the early 1970s. That it got as far as it did was an impressive testament to its capabilities. Loyalism, for its part, found itself on a path that failed almost entirely to find any way to convert its sympathizing constituency into an electorally significant force.

IRA strategy at the end of the 1960s was to delegitimize the Northern Ireland state and government, and this required restraint on its part rather than physical aggression. Nonetheless, non-violent protest as a principle was hardly part of the republican DNA. At the very least, nationalist Catholic communities in Northern Ireland expected armed republicans to serve *in extremis* as a line of defence against loyalist and state attack. The spring and summer of 1969 was a period of loyalist offensive. In some respects, the single most successful paramilitary operation of the entire Troubles was the loyalist bombing of Belfast's water supplies in April 1969, which they allowed to be blamed on republicans. This made Terence O'Neill's continuation as prime minister impossible and, as he recollected in his memoirs, he was 'literally blown out of office'. Thereafter, loyalist pressure mostly came in the form of riotous incursion into Catholic residential areas. This reached a devastating climacteric in August 1969.

In Derry, the Catholic Bogside rioted against the traditional loyalist Apprentice Boys' parade. Within hours, barricades were thrown up and the Bogside found itself besieged by the RUC, with loyalists waiting to follow on. Intense rioting lasted for three days and was only quieted when the British army came on the streets. Much worse was the situation in Belfast, where the RUC, fearing IRA insurrection, ran amok in Catholic west Belfast, followed by loyalist mobs. Hundreds of Catholic families were burned out of their homes. It was a high point for loyalism. 'The Union Jack was planted in the middle of the Falls Road that night,' John McKeague of the Shankill Defence Association recalled with satisfaction in 1972. 'Something that had never happened before—it could happen again.'

The IRA policy in 1969 was still restraint and though it did play an important role in area defence, and to a limited extent deployed weapons in the besieged Catholic ghettos of Belfast, they were nowhere near strong enough to protect against large-scale forced expulsions of Catholics by loyalist crowds. A growing revolt against the leadership's 'popular front' strategy was catalysed and at the end of 1969 and the beginning of 1970 both the IRA and Sinn Féin split. The Provisional IRA condemned the official leadership as hopelessly compromised by its flirtation with communism and rededicated itself to traditionalist and militarist republicanism.

The Provisionals soon found themselves playing a leading role in the Catholic ghetto defence organizations which continued to organize behind the barricades that had been thrown up in August 1969. Elements of the establishment in independent Ireland, anxious to help organize northern communities for self-defence, found Provisional affiliates easier to work with than far-left Official IRA representatives. When the British government loudly protested against southern Irish intervention the Catholic ghettos found themselves isolated and they increasingly turned to the IRA, which had long experience in arms smuggling, training a disciplined cadre, and organizing counter-state structures. The Provisional IRA in particular attracted large numbers of northern Catholics anxious to defend their communities in the event of renewed loyalist attack.

Nonetheless, the importance of 'defence' as a reason for joining the IRA has almost certainly been exaggerated. There were, after all, alternative means, each residential area in Belfast having its own defence association and organizations such as the Catholic Ex-Servicemen's Association. Both the Provisional and the Official IRA were quite clear that they were *offensive* organizations, committed to overthrowing the state in Northern Ireland, and reuniting the country of Ireland by force. Their propaganda generally played down simple 'defence' as both inadequate and inherently sectarian. Certainly there was a gap, particularly in the Provisional IRA, between the Dublin-based leadership and the northern rank and file. To some extent this can be seen in the newspapers of the Provisionals: *An Phoblacht* in the South emphasized the traditional republican language of the 'common name of Irishmen' while *Republican News* in the North was much more explicit in championing the 'Catholic' community against both loyalism and the British state. Nonetheless, the principal enemy was defined at the outset as 'British imperialism' and specifically the British army in Northern Ireland.

Though the trigger for joining the IRA was usually some perceived immediate injustice, such as loyalist attack or British army brutality, the necessary background was a particular historical sense. As one early Provisional recruit, Shane O'Doherty, put it,

My attraction to the IRA was not initially based on the sight or experience of any particular social injustice, though, when I did join the IRA, injustices were foremost in my motivation. It was the discovery of the tragedies of Irish history which first caused my desire to give myself to the IRA, and the best part of that history I imbibed alone at home reading books I found in the family library. It was the pure political injustice and tragedy of British rule in Ireland against the wishes of the Irish people which fired my anger, not forgetting the Famine and mass emigration.

Provisional IRA 'Volunteers' were not, as a rule, traumatized by stressors, but psychologically stable. They were well integrated into a multigenerational tradition, with about 80 per cent having fathers, uncles, or brothers in the movement.

Even in the earliest days considerable efforts were made to train recruits in a particular 'cadre ideology' which laid stress on centuries of resistance to British rule, the achievements of the IRA in the War of Independence and their betrayal by 'politicians', the illegitimacy of both partition states on either side of the border, even the fantastic notion that the IRA's 'Army Council' was the direct inheritor of the first Irish Republic, established in 1916 and confirmed in the general elections of 1918 and 1920, and so still the legitimate government of Ireland. This cadre ideology should not be taken entirely seriously on its own terms; it was less a summation of what republicans really believed and understood, more a dogmatic formula that bound together a self-conscious vanguard and justified recourse to lethal violence in a social and moral context that otherwise would have forbidden such enormities. It must be recalled that for most of its existence the IRA was on ceasefire and even in its most militarist phase in the 1970s, the Provisional IRA were always alive to the importance of the ceasefire as an inevitable part of their struggle.

Both the Official and the Provisional IRA defined the phase of operations in which they were involved in 1970 as having passed beyond that of non-violent protest to violent 'defence' against loyalist and army attacks on Catholic–nationalist areas. They were quite explicit that this was preparatory to an offensive against the structures of British imperialism as they saw it. 'Defence' was both a pressing need and the most permissive context for recruitment, organization, and training. Under pressure from the Unionists at Stormont, which the British army was striving to shore up, the army from the election of the Conservative government in June 1970 adopted a more coercive approach against Catholic ghettos, seeking to sweep them of arms and self-defence structures which they saw, not unreasonably, as increasingly intertwined with an IRA cadre committed to the revolutionary use of violence.

Loyalist paramilitaries continued their campaign of violence, harassment, and where possible expulsion of exposed Catholic communities, particularly in Belfast. Recognizing the primary anti-state threat as coming from the IRA, the British army paid relatively little attention to loyalist violence, which in turn did its best to act in concert with the army. The Provisional IRA won particular kudos in late June 1970 when it was involved in the defence of the Short Strand area of Belfast against loyalist mobs in a battle that the army refused to involve itself in. When, under pressure from the Unionist government at Stormont, the British army in July 1970 conducted a mass raid on the Official IRA stronghold of the Lower Falls Road, imposing a dubiously legal curfew on the area, the militancy of the Provisional IRA received a considerable boost. Marie Drumm, a female leader of Provisional Sinn Féin, organized a 'march of mothers' from all over West Belfast to bring food, and particularly milk and baby food, into the Falls Road. As Joe Cahill, a senior member of the Provisional IRA, recalled, 'The same prams used to carry in food were used to take out a considerable number of weapons, handed over by people who were in danger of being caught in possession. The women brought the food in and brought the guns out.'

The Provisional IRA held its own Volunteers back, seeking first to build up a constituency in the Catholic areas habituated to riotous battling against the army. The fire-breathing elements of the Provisionals strained at the leash, shown most dramatically by the unauthorized murder of three young and off-duty Scots soldiers in March 1971. By early 1971, the Provisional IRA had moved from 'defence' to 'defence-retaliation'. The Official IRA, preferring to think of itself as an elite force autonomous from the street, focused upon high-profile, high-prestige attacks, but in so doing they only managed to violate the evolving norms of toleration for violence in the Catholic areas. The killing of Unionist Senator Barnhill in December 1971, during an attempt to take over and demolish his house, and the bombing of Aldershot Barracks in the aftermath of Bloody Sunday in 1972—an overly complicated operation that managed simply to kill six women canteen workers and a Roman Catholic chaplain—were propaganda disasters for the Officials, and their morale for offensive operations quickly diminished. The Provisional IRA, in contrast, reserved its complex operations for gun-running and bomb production, otherwise allowing its Volunteers freedom to engage with the British army as they encountered them on the streets.

The Provisionals in 1971 launched a sustained bombing campaign against commercial targets in Belfast and other city and town centres, the idea being to generalize a sense of crisis across the province of while drawing the British army away from Catholic ghettos where the IRA were organizing. In response the British army rather unwillingly agreed to a proposal from Stormont that internment—arrest without trial—be introduced. Operation Demetrius in August 1971 was the initial swoop, based upon poor intelligence. Clearly it unleashed the aggression of the army, which had been increasingly frustrated in its inconclusive encounters with a shadowy enemy. The Ballymurphy Massacre in Belfast, August 1971 (seven civilians killed), and Bloody Sunday in Derry, January 1972 (thirteen civilians killed), more or less definitively crushed out mass riotous mobilization on the street, a natural response to the British government's acknowledgement of actual war with the IRA in July 1971.

This was the period of all-out armed struggle by the Provisional IRA, in which its members and resources were thrown into a campaign of opportunity, and attacks were to be as numerous as possible. As the Provisionals' Chief-of-Staff Seán Mac Stíofáin recalled, 'From internment on, UDR and RUC personnel, like British soldiers, were treated as legitimate combatant targets at all times, whether on duty or not, armed or not, in uniform or not.' The main examples followed by the Provisionals were the guerrilla campaigns against the British in Cyprus in the 1950s and Aden in the 1960s. Algeria was not a direct model, because of the indiscriminate civilian casualties the FLN caused. 'Set-pieces' were relatively rare, and prone to backfire when attempted. The attempt in July 1972 to set off twenty bombs against commercial targets within minutes in and around the centre of Belfast misfired when panic meant that their warnings proved insufficient. Civilian casualties were high (nine dead, 130 injured) and the day became notorious as Bloody Friday.

On the whole, however, the Provisional IRA fought a relatively constrained campaign. Their targets of choice were first of all British army personnel on the streets of Northern Ireland, secondly locally recruited security forces such as the RUC and UDR. These were 'hard targets' and there was considerable degree of effort to avoid civilian casualties (though there was a cynical calculation that collateral damage was inevitable). The IRA thought of itself as a guerrilla army rather than terrorist. They did not adopt a nihilistic death cult ideology characteristic of 21st-century Islamist terrorism. Nor did they have a millenarian ambition for societal reconstruction on the morrow of victory: they were neither fascist nor genuinely revolutionary socialist.

Discussions of the Provisional IRA in the 1970s have been dominated, ironically, by their Official IRA rivals, who called a ceasefire in 1972. The Officials made a point of denigrating the political capacity of the Provisionals and emphasizing their apolitical militarism. From a rival organization that prided itself on its Marxist-Leninist rigour, this was an unsurprising allegation. It was reinforced in later years, however, by the Provisionals' own 'northern leadership', led by Martin McGuinness and Gerry Adams, who replaced the disgraced Dublin-based leadership of Dáithí Ó Conaill and Seán Mac Stíofáin who had led the organization in the 1970s. Adams et al. had their own factional reasons to exaggerate the political innocence of the Provisional IRA in its militarily most successful period. Certainly, the Provisionals were not a sophisticated political operation in the 1970s. But it is going too far to deny any kind of political strategy on their part.

The Provisional strategy from about 1971 to 1974 can be described as 'controlled maximum targeted force'. It was maximum in that the IRA recruited as fast as possible and threw its members into armed actions at every opportunity. It was targeted in that uniformed members of the security forces were the defined enemy. It was controlled in that the IRA wished to demonstrate that it could turn violence on and off at will. The strategy used force as a bargaining counter to send the message that a genuine willingness to negotiate by Britain would lead to a cessation of republican violence.

The Provisionals were always aware that they could not win on military terms alone. They would always be outgunned. Nor did they believe that active militarism was a good in itself. After all, for most of their existence they had been in a state of ceasefire. The IRA had at least a modicum of understanding that unionists had interests that could not be entirely overlooked. They had long adopted the position agreed by the Second Dáil Éireann, that the six counties of Northern Ireland should retain their devolved governmental structure, though owing allegiance to Irish rather than British sovereignty. By 1970, this had evolved into the policy of *Éire Nua*, a proposed confederation for the new Ireland including a government for the nine counties of historic Ulster (which would dilute the unionist majority). Barely any unionist took this at all seriously, but *Éire Nua* at least recognized that partition would have to be undermined politically as well as by armed force. The republican movement made fairly serious attempts to establish a parallel representative assembly for nine-county Ulster, Dáil Ulaid, in 1970–1, though ultimately it was drowned out by the din of armed struggle and the SDLP's establishment of an ephemeral 'Assembly of the North' as an avowed talking shop. The Provisionals were certainly aware of the need for a political strategy, but without a strong political wing to the movement, the nurturing of which would necessarily detract from the all-out campaign of armed struggle the IRA prioritized in the 1970s, they were unable to make a breakthrough.

A revolutionary organization has by definition bold and far-reaching aims. It is always likely to do better, however, if it sets itself achievable intermediate goals. In the early 1970s, the Provisional IRA had three. Its first aim was to bring down Stormont. This was achievable, and Stormont fell in March 1972. It is certainly the case that Stormont had been in peril since the outbreak of the civil rights movement, and it was Britain's disaffection with the Unionist government that was the proximate cause of its downfall. But it is very difficult to imagine that Stormont would have been prorogued without the pressure of the IRA campaign.

Secondly, the IRA wanted to bring Britain to negotiation. This was also achievable, as William Whitelaw, the Secretary of State for Northern Ireland, agreed a truce and opened up negotiations with the IRA in July 1972. It is generally considered that the IRA went into these talks with completely unrealistic expectations, dictating to Britain as if to a defeated enemy, and demanding nothing but British withdrawal. However, there was only one meeting of both sides, and it is hardly surprising that IRA negotiators—a team including Gerry Adams and Martin McGuinness—started high with a demand for a British Declaration of Intent to Withdraw. This is a normal negotiating strategy. It is quite clear from other evidence, however, that the Provisional IRA were expecting a lengthy multi-party process: 'neutrally convened talks' at a 'conference of Irish organisations of all politics and denominations actively involved in the situation in the North', as Seán Mac Stíofáin put it. They were looking for a 'place at a conference on the future of Ireland', agreed Maria Maguire, an observer then privy to the IRA's leadership thinking. This is not to say that the republicans were particularly realistic in expecting this to resolve with a United Ireland even in the medium term. But it is wrong to assume that they were entirely politically naive.

As the third intermediate aim, the Provisional IRA wished to frustrate any attempted settlement by the British which would exclude them. This meant, following the rapid collapse of the July 1972 ceasefire, that the Provisionals had an incentive to maintain maximal armed pressure in an attempt to sabotage Britain's subsequent attempt to negotiate a settlement that sidelined republicans. This was also a realistic aim. For the next two years, Britain chivvied the constitutional parties into agreeing a power-sharing settlement while making no substantial concessions on its campaign against the IRA. The resulting Sunningdale Agreement was given no chance by the IRA to stabilize and it was brought down by a loyalist strike in 1974. As the IRA must have expected, Britain then turned wearily back to negotiations with the IRA.

They sped this up, or so they hoped, with terrible attacks in Great Britain which, at the far limit of effective command and control, were even more likely to inflict atrocity. The November 1974 Birmingham pub bombings wreaked most devastation at the Tavern in the Town, an underground venue. Many were killed not by the blast but by the inferno of 2000° heat. One girl was blinded by pieces of bone from a man's skull. The suspects for this attack who were picked up by the police, brutalized, and forced into confession were, as it turned out, innocent. These horrors played some role in persuading Britain to recognize a truce with the IRA in 1975.

The rationale behind loyalist violence

The aims lying behind loyalist paramilitary violence were simpler than those of the IRA. Rather than seeking to force change, loyalists saw themselves as bolstering a status quo that was already defended by the forces of the state. However, the British army was an instrument of a government in London which, from the loyalist point of view, was less than wholeheartedly committed to the Union. The RUC and Ulster Defence Regiment were 'politically sound', broadly speaking (a secret British report in 1973 estimated that 5–15 per cent of UDR soldiers were members of loyalist paramilitaries), but ultimately under the control of the British government. Loyalist violence was first and foremost designed to place pressure on British policy-making. It was based on a kind of 'risk theory' in which the function of loyalist violence was to clearly demonstrate that Britain would be taking the risk of a catastrophically violent reaction from the Protestant majority in Northern Ireland if it seriously contemplated selling out the Union. In this sense, loyalist violence was not directed against the IRA head-on. Rather, it was to serve as a counterbalance, limiting Britain's room for manoeuvre.

Loyalism's targeting strategy was radically different from that of the IRA. It attacked almost exclusively Catholic civilians. This served a purpose in confirming the message that British withdrawal could only result in a sectarian bloodbath. Between August 1969 and the proroguing of Stormont in 1972, loyalist violence generally took the form of expelling Catholics from areas defined as Protestant. With the fall of Stormont, however, it quickly turned into death squad activity aimed at Catholic civilians. For about a year, the security forces refused to recognize that a loyalist campaign was in existence, defining numerous Catholic deaths as 'motiveless murders'.

Politically speaking, loyalists were generally uncreative. As a broadly working-class movement, they tended to share the Labourist class-consciousness and social solidarity ethic of the trade union organized working class in Great Britain. There was also a heavy dose of the toxic masculinity, xenophobic hostility to outsiders, and social illiberalism that characterized the traditional Tory working class. *Loyalist News* in 1974 referred to Catholic rioters as 'these white Negroes... sub-creatures'. Outright fascists were never absent from loyalism, but generally speaking it was politically conformist in its ideals, seeking a majoritarian democracy and preferential benefit for 'the people' (defined as loyal Protestants) rather than theocracy, anti-Catholic apartheid, or anything of a radically right-wing description.

The human material that loyalist paramilitaries could draw upon was generally unimpressive, given the alternative attractions of legitimate security forces such as the RUC and the UDR, and there existed a disproportionately high percentage of people with psychopathic tendencies or personality disorders within loyalism. As a loyalist remembered: 'From mid July 1972 the Shankill was the place to be. Many Catholics were picked up as they passed through the fringes of the district and brought to romper rooms for interrogation. ['Romper rooms', named after a children's programme popular at the time, were usually pub basements set aside for torture.] Once they were caught, their lives were over. How easily or how cruelly they died, depended on which squad captured them. Some would be dead within an hour; others would die a slow and very painful death.' The sadistic Shankill Butchers gang, active between 1975 and 1982 and responsible for killing at least twenty-three people, was only the most notorious loyalist death squad.

Nonetheless, around these death squads was a much larger and capable network, with considerable organizational acumen developed in the Northern Ireland labour movement and the marching orders. This loyalist 'community' was particularly effective in working-class communities and the workplace. The loyalists, through the Ulster Workers Council, were able to call and sustain a nine-day general strike in 1974 which brought down the British-brokered Sunningdale settlement. It was the most effective political strike in British history.

The UWC victory inaugurated a period of loyalist dominance. It was certainly helped by an element of state collusion. The mid-Ulster 'Glennane Gang', an informal alliance between the Ulster Volunteer Force and members of both the RUC and UDR, active in the 1970s, has since been identified by Anne Cadwallader and others. This organization killed about 120 people, only one of whom could be identified as an active republican. Generally speaking, members of the security forces who aided or acted as loyalist paramilitaries were sheltered from pursuit and conviction. When in 1980 a number were given strikingly lenient sentences by the Chief Justice, Lord Lowry, this most senior judge on the Northern Ireland bench explained himself by saying that the defendants understandably felt 'that more than ordinary police work was needed and was justified to rid the land of the pestilence which has been in existence'. He declared that when it came to violation of the law by members of the security forces he would always impose punishment 'on a different and lower scale from that appropriate to terrorists'. This winking at collusion was a substantial organizational asset for loyalist paramilitarism.

The Peace People

In hardened working-class republican areas, the section of the population identified by a British army document as 'decent people' most likely to 'oust the gunmen and terrorists' were 'women over 30' who 'genuinely fear for their children'.

On 10 August 1976, two children, aged 4 weeks and 8 years, were killed when a car swerved out of control, crushing them and their mother and brother against some railings on Finaghy Road North, Belfast. The IRA driver of the car had been shot dead at the wheel during an exchange of fire with pursuing troops. A third child died later. Two days later, more than 1,000 women gathered at the spot where the three children had died to protest the tragedy. Women in Andersonstown, a working-class housing estate in Catholic west Belfast, organized a 'Peace People' petition against violence which collected some 6,000 signatures. The next day, over 10,000 people attended a peace rally. Hymns were sung, and several busloads of women from the fiercely loyalist Shankill Road attended.

This was impressive and moving. Two problems were immediately apparent, however. After the rally, Provisional sympathizers harassed and abused those attending. Meanwhile, in Whitecross, County Armagh, a 12-year-old girl was shot dead by the army. The politics of the latest atrocity gradually dissipated the shock value of the originating horror.

Nevertheless, the peace movement continued to develop. On 21 August, about 20,000 people attended a peace rally in Ormeau Park, Belfast. At the gathering, one of the organizers, Mrs Mairéad Corrigan (Figure 6), the aunt of the three children killed on 10 August, appealed to the people of the North to 'come out and show the world they want peace'. People from all over Belfast took part. There followed substantial marches on the Shankill Road, in Lurgan, Bangor, Armagh, Derry, Newry, and Dublin. This was a genuine mass movement.

The republican movement was rattled. Máire Drumm, vice-president of Provisional Sinn Féin, accused the women's peace movement of being pro-British, anti-republican, and funded by the British. The government declined to offer the Peace People official backing because this might help its detractors, but rather

6. Betty Williams and Mairéad Corrigan at the first meeting of the Peace People in Andersonstown, Belfast, August 1976. Provisional IRA supporters were highly embarrassed and a contemporary article in Republican News, discreetly written in Irish, criticized Andersonstown, with its proportion of private housing, as tainted by the middle class: 'there will always be a division between Republicans and a large section of the people of this area'.

spoiled the effect by linking it to a rise of 12 per cent in use of the confidential telephone line, a facility that allowed citizens to discreetly inform on paramilitary activities. The DUP, for its part, accused the women's peace movement of being 'counter-productive' because it was 'diverting attention from winning the war against the IRA'.

The peace marches had much in common with those of the civil rights era, similarly borrowing techniques of passive resistance and the protest song 'We Shall Overcome' from the Black freedom movement in the USA. However, the marchers faced aggression and violence from youngsters—'they must have been babes in arms when these Troubles started', remarked one peace activist. On 10 October 1976, at a tenants' meeting in the Catholic Turf Lodge to protest against the death of a Catholic boy (13) struck on the head by an Army plastic bullet, three peace leaders came under physical attack.

As the Peace People moved from simple protests to political engagement, they came under fire from the previously supportive SDLP. Ivan Cooper accused its leadership of time-wasting with self-aggrandizing 'irrelevancies' such as publicity trips abroad. Paddy Devlin of the same party attacked the Peace People for 'going political'. Indeed, on 6 January 1977, the Peace People issued an ambitious six-page document entitled *Strategy for Peace*. It envisaged an 'assembly' of non-party groups which would elect an 'executive': 'a form of government hopefully to solve Northern Ireland's problems', as its author Ciaran McKeown put it. Irritated at this political adventurism and McKeown's scornful attitude to the Catholic community's leaders, Peace People branches in Belfast's Andersonstown and Derry split away. 'The Peace People's job is not to criticise politicians, or party politics, churchmen or Churches, community workers or associations,' said the dissenters. The movement had effectively lost its working-class base.

In 1977 Mairéad Corrigan and Betty Williams, leaders of the Peace People, were awarded the Nobel Peace Prize. But this was really a last hurrah. The executive committee of the Peace People was soon mired in internecine disputes, both personal and on the issue of paramilitary prisoners' rights. Betty Williams, one of the founder-members, announced her resignation in February 1980. Those dissenting groups which had split in 1977, however, were to play a significant background role in facilitating the emerging Irish republican peace process in the 1980s.

Paramilitarism, if anything, consolidated as a 'way of life'. By 1980 two-thirds of those serving sentences of over four years had been under 10 years old when the Troubles began in 1969. While patriotic enthusiasm was more or less common to men and women, however, males were far more likely to participate in violent paramilitarism than females (and were far more likely to be victims). The strain was felt by partners and children. 'While Colette made a home, Paddy fought a sporadic war,' wrote Nell McCafferty of one republican family in Derry. 'They would quarrel about this, he would attempt to settle down, and then he would be off soldiering again... "Colette, I miss the IRA." He said he could never live without it; he had to be in it; he said it was the only thing that made sense with the war going on.' Sally Belfrage, who explored Belfast society for a year in the mid-1980s, felt moved to accept it 'as one of those mysteries forever beyond my understanding: something about being a boy, about establishing and asserting an identity among men, about power and aggressiveness, about belonging'. A few years later, Pastor Jack McGee and Roy Montgomery of the Shankill Road told the Opsahl Inquiry that

> Paramilitaries are as much a way of life in working class communities in North and West Belfast as the Boys Brigade and the Boy Scouts would be in other cities... and for many people they can aspire to nothing higher in life than to be accepted into the ranks. To be 'one of the boys' is to be regarded as someone of importance... Paramilitary leaders, past and present, are, generally speaking, revered by the young and considered to be working class heroes.

As Northern Ireland painfully deindustrialized, alternatives for young working-class males were not obvious. By 1983, unemployment was running at 20.4 per cent overall, 26.4 per cent for males. Lord Gowrie, Minister of State at the Northern Ireland Office, concluded gloomily that Northern Ireland was heading for a long-term level of about 25 per cent male unemployment, which would be well over 40 per cent in some areas. By late 1987, in fact, it reached an astonishing 27.6 per cent of the workforce. West Belfast endured over 50 per cent youth unemployment. Economic misery was a seedbed for paramilitarism (Figure 7).

7. 'Out of the Ashes rose the Provisionals.' Gable wall murals, an old Orange tradition, began to be painted in republican areas from around the time of the 1981 hunger strikes.

The IRA and the 'Long War'

Loyalist violence ensured that the 1975 Truce negotiations between the Provisional IRA and the British government would go nowhere. It seems likely that the British side in these contacts were attempting to entice republicanism into the political sphere. Republicans were allowed to establish incident centres, to facilitate coordination between the IRA and the British government in maintaining the ceasefire. Sinn Féin was legalized. The British government had perhaps hoped that the emergence of a working-class politics of the extremes, loyalism on the one side and republicanism on the other, would create the conditions in which Northern Ireland could be pushed to the furthest extremity of the Union, preparatory for its ultimate transfer to an all-Ireland sovereignty. Loyalist violence was certainly sufficient to make clear that any such dramatic experimentation would go awry. A demoralized IRA drifted towards out-and-out sectarianism, occasionally using *noms de guerre*, as in the notorious Kingsmill massacre of ten Protestant workers in south Armagh in January 1976.

Republicans had come to realize that the British government was not willing to take any risks with the situation in Northern Ireland so long as the 'loyalist backlash' was so obviously a threat. The IRA was now faced with a conundrum. There was no longer a credible intermediary aim for their violence—Stormont was gone, there was no British orchestrated settlement to destabilize, and negotiations had led nowhere. A cessation of the armed struggle, however, would simply dissipate all the sacrifices made up to this point. The political wing of republicanism was in no fit state to carry the republican cause alone. It was, moreover, quite the worst time to call a ceasefire. In 1972, the IRA could have ended its armed struggle with a sense of having fought a 'good war' and won considerable concessions. But in the circumstances of 1975–6, an indefinite cessation of violence would simply have looked like a generational defeat with the politics of the republican movement heavily besmirched by overt sectarian degeneration.

The IRA instead adopted the strategy of the 'Long War'. As they put it in 1978:

> The Republican Movement considers that for both political and economic reasons the British remain extremely determined to hang on to the six occupied counties. Therefore owing entirely to this British intransigence the war to liberate and unify this country will be a bitter and long drawn-out struggle. There is no quick solution to our British problem.

The 'Long War' orientation, developed from 1977, was based upon the assumption that for the foreseeable future the British government would take no political initiative likely to dangerously alienate loyalist opinion. Instead, Britain would seek simply to contain the violence in Northern Ireland in the hope that the IRA would see no purpose in continuing. In due course, Britain calculated, violence would fade away. It was the intention of the IRA, therefore, to show that it would not fade. 'Ireland unfree would never be at peace.' Britain must come to accept that political violence would be endemic in Northern Ireland unless and until it grasped the nettle and offered substantial concessions to nationalism.

The Long War required a reconfiguration of republican 'cadre ideology'. In the absence of intermediary strategic aims, the focus turned to consolidating and sustaining the republican vanguard. This meant a policy of limited recruitment and carefully calibrated violence with the emphasis on minimizing losses through arrests and casualties. It also meant developing a 'social republican' politics of community engagement, activism, feminism, and socialistic ideology, all calculated to buttress a hegemonic counterculture in their working-class bases of support. That this was somewhat lacking was indicated by the rise of the Irish National Liberation Army (INLA) from the mid-1970s and, to a lesser extent, the Irish Independence Party.

Loyalism's dominance came to a sudden end in 1977 when it overreached, launching a second general strike. With less support than the 1974 strike, and a sterner response from the government and army, it collapsed. The violence carried out by loyalism sharply reduced and stayed at a low level until the end of the 1980s. However, the loyalist bluff had been called not in order to facilitate a new settlement, but to preserve a policy of simple containment. Loyalist violence remained at a relatively low level partly because the British government was not seeking to introduce any radically new political initiative. Insofar as loyalism tended to respond to British moves, it had a considerably reduced *raison d'être* from 1975.

The hunger strikes

A logical corollary of Britain's containment strategy—attrition to wear the IRA down—was a radical change in its prisons policy. Internees, by legal definition, were guilty of no proven offence, so naturally they were not treated as convicts. Instead they were allowed freedom of association, dress, and spare time within the grim internment camps. With convictions a relatively unimportant element of the counterinsurgency strategy in the early 1970s, it made little sense to have convicted paramilitary prisoners treated any differently, and as an incentive to the IRA to enter into negotiations in 1972, a Special Category Status, equivalent to internee-rights, had been conceded to paramilitary prisoners held in the regular prison system. A special status for paramilitary prisoners was logical when the expectation was that political violence would be ended by a settlement in the foreseeable future, and that most prisoners would thereupon be released. Once Britain definitively turned to a long-haul criminalization of the republican armed struggle, however, prisoners had to be made to feel that they faced serving whole terms. Prisoner numbers had expanded massively in the early 1970s, and it took some time to erect a penitentiary system adequate to handle them. New prison accommodation, made up of blocks arranged as a capital H for better control, opened up at the Maze Prison site in 1976, the same year internment was phased out. Ciaran Nugent became the first prisoner to be deprived of Special Category Status. Ordered to wear prison uniform, he refused, and so Nugent became the first republican prisoner to protest against the new regime.

Prisoners were a subject close to many hearts in working-class communities. As an indicator, between 1973 and 1990, 14,220 people were charged with paramilitary offences, and 12,087 convicted. Taking into account extended families, this directly impacted on about 100,000 people. Republican prisoners in particular developed a militant esprit de corps, and ironically serving time provided the structures for the organization and politicization of a vanguard not available to 'Volunteers' still at liberty. As the prisoners saw themselves, 'We are not criminals and we are ready and willing to meet an agonising death on hunger strike to establish that we are political prisoners' (1981 Press Release).

Both loyalist and republican prisoners were agreed that the withdrawal of Special Category Status was unjustified. They pointed out that the legal system used to convict them was anything but 'normal'. They were denied jury trials, and there was an extremely heavy reliance upon confessions. This was all the more controversial given revelations regarding the beating of suspects at the RUC's Castlereagh Holding Centre. There is not much evidence that many prisoners were innocent of involvement in paramilitary violence. However, it was clear that they were in practice being treated as combatants.

The struggle in and around the prisons was grotesquely lethal. Prisoners, in refusing to wear uniforms and wary of leaving their cells for fear of beatings, took to smearing their excrement on their walls. This became known as the 'dirty protest'. Prison warders were also in a grim situation, frustrated and often violent in the midst of human degradation, and suffering real terror in the face of a murder campaign. Cardinal Tomás Ó Fiaich described conditions for the 300 or so protesting prisoners as 'hardly fit for animals'. A Report by the European Commission of Human Rights, published in June 1980, agreed that the condition of protesting prisoners was 'almost sub-human', but insisted that this was 'self-inflicted': 'designed to create maximum sympathy and to enlist public support for their political aims'. It did, however, counsel more flexibility from the British government.

Though both loyalists and republican prisoners favoured political status they did not cooperate in their campaigns to achieve this. The prison protests quickly became a trial of strength between the

British administration and republican prisoners. Ruairí Ó Brádaigh, President of Sinn Féin, described the issue as 'a showdown with imperialism'. Republicans would not deign to work with loyalists in this struggle and loyalists would not aid their enemy against British authority.

The prison protests proved to be a singular opportunity for the IRA. In 1976, Máire Drumm, Vice-President of Sinn Féin, warned that Belfast would 'come down stone by stone' in the struggle for special category status. This was obviously an exaggeration. But the prisons issue did demonstrate that the British strategy of containment was based upon a false premise. Republicans were able to sustain a baseline level of crisis that could of itself erupt into acute phases even without Britain poking the hornets' nest. The prisons issue, therefore, was ideal from a republican point of view in demonstrating to Britain that the situation in Northern Ireland would not spontaneously pacify if only Britain remorselessly bore down on nationalist insurgency. The republican hope was that Britain would be forced to readjust its calculus and reconsider the merits of a political initiative that would risk unionist and loyalist reaction, if that was the price required to buy off republican violence. However, first of all republicans had to win a success in the prisons. Margaret Thatcher, the British Prime Minister, had after all defined the prison protests as the 'last throw of the dice' by the IRA.

Almost inevitably, therefore, prison protests escalated to the ultimate weapon of hunger strike, abortively in 1980 and then fatally—ten men dead on hunger strike—in 1981. This produced in Bobby Sands perhaps the only genuine folk hero of the modern republican struggle. He was an interestingly non-macho character, physically slight and poetically inclined, but with an iron determination to have every captured IRA Volunteer recognized as a 'well-trained and competent soldier, a versatile and deadly guerrilla fighter'.

Women were deeply involved in the prisons issue: directly at Armagh Prison (though they were forbidden to join the second hunger strike) and hardly less directly as the main family support. Women bore the brunt of keeping in touch with prisoners, visiting, looking after dependants. Marriages often broke up on prisoners' release.

Female prisoners were a small minority, but perhaps felt the pressure even more. Judith Ward, a mentally ill woman wrongfully convicted of a savage IRA bombing in Great Britain in 1974, which killed nine soldiers and three civilians, remembered the double-standard applied to female convicts:

> The 'bad' women are punished more severely for their crimes than their male counterparts, particularly crimes of violence, it being seen as so unnatural that women should have perpetrated such acts. The 'mad' ones may get off more lightly but are often consigned to a psychiatric dustbin where their behaviour is, in an almost patronising way, explained by the hormones or age.

Sister Sarah Clarke, active in helping Irish suspects in Great Britain, was shocked at what she took to be the bias of the judicial system, and noted disapprovingly how judges would 'huff, puff and roll...eyes during the defence summing up'. Some of the more shocking miscarriages of justice, indeed, took place in Great Britain, most notoriously the unfair conviction for atrocious IRA bombings of the Guildford Four and the Birmingham Six.

The prison conflict in Northern Ireland was deeply embittered and violent. Brutality by the warders was well attested to, but they suffered horrible attrition themselves. By 1985, twenty-five prison warders had been assassinated, including the assistant governor of the Maze Prison. On the day Bobby Sands died, on the sixty-sixth day of his fast, rioting spread across republican areas. Derek McWeeney (45) and his 15-year-old son Desmond were fatally injured when their milk float was pelted with bricks by a crowd supporting the hunger strikes. Over the course of the strike, 51 people died violently, more than 1,000 were injured, and 1,700 were arrested.

The hunger strike was called off without any overt British concessions. But in most senses, the hunger strikes proved to be a republican triumph. As Dáithí Ó Conaill said,

> The reality was that ten men had the courage to stand by their country to the point of giving their lives for it, and that was the real victory....As a result they wiped out during the hunger strike British claims that these were mindless hooligans.

In the years following, special category status effectively re-evolved in the prisons. By the 1990s, it was acknowledged that prisoners took their orders not from warders, but from paramilitary commanders on the wings.

The ballot box and the Armalite

The hunger strikes proved to be the ideal situation for launching Sinn Féin as an electoral vehicle, at last rounding out the strategy of the Long War. Even before the strike ended, Sinn Féin said it would contest future Northern Ireland elections. In the general election of 1983 they won 102,701 votes, 13.6 per cent of the total, a level they would not surpass until 1997. This move towards the ballot box had consequences for the Provisionals' discourse, which increasingly adopted a paradoxical ideology of 'human rights'. Nonetheless, armed struggle remained key to the strategy, and there was no hurry to enter into negotiations.

The shift in IRA 'cadre ideology' meant that the use of violence was becoming increasingly problematic. Even during the heightened passions of the hunger strikes, the IRA did not throw open its doors to new members as it had done in the 1970s. Instead the IRA was to act as the cutting edge of a broader republican constituency. This was partly a response to improved security force capabilities in waging calibrated counterinsurgency. Most notable, perhaps, was the introduction of 'Improved Northern Ireland Body Armour', which gave the security forces unprecedented protection against sniping attacks. The IRA were increasingly reduced either to doorstep assassinations, mostly against locally recruited forces or even civilian contractors, or enormous bombs and exceptionally high powered rifles which could only be used in country districts if unacceptable risk to civilians was to be avoided. Technically sophisticated attacks had their inevitable concomitant civilian casualties, as with the November 1987 Remembrance Day bombing in Enniskillen, which killed twelve people when the explosives went off prematurely. Bold but risky overseas operations were planned. Mairéad Farrell, who had joined the IRA after a school friend was blinded by a British army rubber bullet, was arrested in 1976 and became leader of the protesting republican prisoners at Armagh during the prison protests. She returned to 'active service' upon release and became a leading IRA operator. In March 1988 she was shot along with two other IRA Volunteers by British soldiers in controversial circumstances while leading a bombing reconnaissance in Gibraltar. This reflected a harder-line security force posture just within the limits of Yellow Card rules of engagement. The security forces deliberately organized interception operations which allowed them to take out IRA units with arms in hand. At the Loughgall ambush in May 1987, security forces shot to death an entire IRA unit of eight men, plus one unfortunate passer-by.

Nonetheless, IRA capacity remained robust and in important respects developed. Their engineering department produced a directional Mark 12 mortar which was able to rain bombs down on 10 Downing Street in February 1991. Massive lorry bombs—'city destroyers'—wreaked devastation in the City of London in 1992/13—at a cost to Britain of $3 billion—and tore out the centre of Manchester in 1996. Back in Northern Ireland, IRA operations were increasingly sophisticated against a now well-attuned security system. In September 1992, a £3,000 IRA bomb destroyed the police Forensic Science Laboratory and much of the evidence therein. Overall, however, the IRA was being constrained in its ambition to maintain a continuous rumble of multilevel attacks. As Gerry Bradley of the IRA recalled, 'the number of ops was down...because the pressure was on us not to injure civilians....It was a matter of pride to get around all the technology the Brits had and still not hurt any civilian....You always erred on the side of doubt. We planned loads of stuff that never got anywhere.' Increasingly the IRA looked less like an 'army of the people', engaging in rumbustiously free-form street battles, and more like a highly secretive, if unquestionably professional, terrorist organization.

The impact of the Anglo-Irish Agreement

The Anglo-Irish Agreement of 1985, which gave the Irish government rights of consultation in the administration of Northern Ireland, was sold by both governments as an anti-Sinn Féin manoeuvre, the better to pass muster with outraged unionist opinion. As Thatcher attempted to combine the agreement with a final attempt to militarily defeat the IRA, republicans seriously considered an attempt to break the deadlock by upping their violence in dramatic form: a 'Tet Offensive' in which republicans would organize a mass breakout of prisoners from the Maze Prison, seize strongholds, and openly challenge the security forces to a very televisual combat. This strategy of all-or-nothing threatened catastrophic defeat and elements within the IRA clearly passed information, allowing the security forces to capture substantial supplies of weapons from the Gaddafi dictatorship in Libya which were meant to provision the operation. The Tet Offensive was called off. But for the republican leadership this was by no means an unmitigated disaster. They were having second thoughts about the significance of the Anglo-Irish Agreement.

In actual fact, as Garret FitzGerald pointed out, the agreement had a second and very deliberately positive message for republican ears—that the two governments were prepared to call the unionist bluff. Nonetheless, at least in the first instance, republicans were opposed to the agreement. They agreed with Charlie Haughey that it was 'copper-fastening partition'. As ever, however, loyalism reacted more to British perfidy than republicanism as such. And after a long period of desuetude it was violently reactivated by the fears for the Union instilled by the agreement. Loyalist paramilitary leaders under the partial control of British intelligence were sloughed off, and for a period there was greater cooperation between the loyalist paramilitary fringe and unionist mainstream than had been seen since Sunningdale. For the first time, in the late 1980s, the number of loyalist killings exceeded that of republicans.

The peace process

The republican strategy of combining the 'Armalite with a ballot box' reached a dead end with the southern Irish election of February 1987. Their derisory vote of 1.9 per cent clearly revealed that association with violence was an absolute barrier to any electoral breakthrough in the republic. In the same year, they lost about 20,000 votes in the Westminster general election contests in Northern Ireland, falling to 11.4 per cent of the total. Sinn Féin's ambition of becoming a powerful and importantly all-Ireland force looked hopeless. The message delivered by the Anglo-Irish Agreement, moreover, was gradually percolating through. As Danny Morrison remembered, 'We wanted British withdrawal—that's what we were fighting and dying and going to jail for. But we also saw that the [Anglo-Irish] Agreement was a concession, although we were not going to trumpet that. It was a concession because it was a move slightly away from unionists towards nationalists.'

It became clear for the first time since the mid-1970s that the British were prepared to put serious pressure on the unionists to compromise with nationalism. By the 1990s, the IRA was now faced with the choice of whether to seek to profit from such a process. This time, Britain made it clear that republicans would not be left out in the cold. Unlike Sunningdale, the peace process would not be directed against them as such. The risk for republicans, therefore, was that continuing their campaign would appear to be simply self-defeating.

Republicans, however, were well aware that Britain was not prepared to offer any Declaration of Intent to withdraw. They decided to enter into negotiations not with the aim of achieving a certain path to their final goal of a united Ireland, but rather of winning pole position within northern nationalism and setting up for a real breakthrough south of the border. Their aim was to in effect marginalize Britain and to power a political strategy primarily within Ireland. An internal IRA discussion paper leaked in 1993 (the so-called TUAS Document) stated that 'republicans are not prepared to wait around for the British to change... Another front has opened up and we should have the confidence and put in the effort to succeed on that front.'

In order to cash in such benefits of the armed struggle as existed, the republican movement required conditions in which they could be seen to move on with advantage. This Britain was prepared to offer. In the peace process, the political structures were primarily agreed between the Ulster Unionist Party and the SDLP. Republican goals focused upon mutual de-militarization, the withdrawal of the British army from active service in Northern Ireland, the release of prisoners, and standing down of locally recruited security forces from defence of British sovereignty as such. It was arranged that the RUC, transformed into the Police Service of Northern Ireland (PSNI), would hand over 'national' security to the British intelligence services. As British counterinsurgency became an intelligence-led watching brief, so did the IRA. Finally in 2005 the IRA was stood down from active service, though it continued to exist and monitor.

Sinn Féin secured its place as the leading representative of nationalism in the North. Its vote surged to 126,921 in 1997 (16 per cent of the vote), reaching a peak of 175,933 in 2001 (25 per cent). While its absolute vote declined thereafter in less intensely contested elections, its percentage rose to 25.5 by 2010. Sinn Féin turned much of its resources to winning a breakthrough in southern Ireland, where it became a second-rank party of the moderately radical left. In a political culture inherited from the long campaign of violence, Sinn Féin now relied upon dedicated attrition and momentum. Nonetheless, its ultimate aim of United Ireland rested upon population shifts within the North, though it continued to entertain the hope that some Protestants might be won over. In the end, the armed struggle could be seen as successful to the extent that it energized a united-Ireland republicanism within the nationalist constituency and allowed Sinn Féin to become its representative. On the other hand, it certainly hardened unionist opposition to any concession on the border, though there was little evidence that there had ever been much softness on this issue. Taken as a whole, it was rather poor return for the horror, death, and destruction of the 'armed struggle'.

Chapter 4
The political parties

During the violent years of the Troubles, those political parties that disavowed the lethal violence of paramilitaries—both nationalist and unionist—were generally referred to under the useful umbrella term of 'the constitutional parties'. This, however, was something of a term of art. In reality, all political actors in Northern Ireland found themselves in a situation where they tried to turn violence to their political advantage. This should not be simply dismissed as cynicism, hypocrisy, or conspiracy. In a situation where political decisions had consequences that necessarily put life and limb at risk, it was quite impossible to wash one's hands entirely. Unionists, entirely in good faith, could argue that any threat to the link between Great Britain and Northern Ireland would produce a tidal wave of violence and that loyalist murders must be seen, to a degree, as a response to the IRA campaign. Nationalists, for their part, could argue quite justifiably that the absence of a settlement that respected the national aspirations of the minority in Northern Ireland created a sense of discontent and alienation that fostered toleration for republican armed force.

In practice, the 'constitutional parties' were only somewhat constitutional. This could hardly be any other way when it was precisely the constitutional status of Northern Ireland that was at issue. Unionists overthrew a Northern Ireland government in

1974 through a general strike, and organized mass civil disobedience against the Anglo-Irish Agreement of 1985.

The Social Democratic and Labour Party, the representative of most nationalists from its formation in August 1971, opposed internment with a rent and rates strike in early 1970s, and expelled from their party anyone who accepted honours from the Crown. More generally, unionists made clear that they would contemplate rebellion against government if they were forced out of the United Kingdom, while nationalists—even while rejecting physical force—were republican separatists in that they supported an eventual United Ireland.

The options of unionism

During the Stormont years, the priority of unionists had been maintaining control of the parliament and government in the province. By the 1949 Ireland Act, partition could only end by the agreement of Stormont. On top of this, control of local government allowed for the whole panoply of discrimination and gerrymandering that ensured the maintenance of a Protestant electoral and demographic majority. Devolution in Northern Ireland acted as a barrier against interference from Great Britain. The circumstances of 'home rule' in Ulster, therefore, reinforced unionist unity: a single party to operate a more or less democratic one-party state. As soon as the civil rights movement broke out in earnest, however, Britain began to interfere in the administration of Northern Ireland. This interference became something close to command once the British army was introduced to maintain order in August 1969. The formal proroguing of Stormont in 1972, and the introduction of direct rule from London, formalized London's immediate responsibility for governance.

This had consequences. Up until 1968, the system in Northern Ireland was operated by the Unionists to keep the Catholics down, the Protestants in, and the British Government out. But once Britain began pushing the Stormont government to one side, unionist calculations necessarily changed. The aim now must be to influence Britain as the single most important player in the conflict. The question was: how could this best be done?

One approach was to keep close to the British, to act as advisers and confidants, and to trust that London would follow unionist advice. This meant presenting a reasonable and amenable face. By keeping close to British policy-makers, and speaking their language, one could reasonably hope to influence them. The problem with this strategy was that it could make unionists look like a pushover. Britain might well be tempted to make concessions to nationalism, in the hope of pacifying militant republican insurgency, and in the belief that mild-mannered unionists would simply swallow it. An alternative approach was to loudly warn off Britain from irresponsibly meddling or 'selling out' by brash tactics of organized fury, doom-mongering, and even calculated 'unreasonableness'. Such belligerent posturing certainly let Britain know that it could not simply take the Protestants of Ulster for granted, but it carried the risk of destroying British sympathy for the unionist cause.

In short, both strategies—mediation and defiance—had their advantages and their disadvantages. As there was no clear best approach, unionism split. To some extent, the divide followed familiar lines: the 'moderates' were more likely to be Church of Ireland, middle class, and self-consciously 'British'; the 'ultras' were more likely to be Presbyterian, working class or small farmer, and self-consciously 'Ulster' in identity. But these were rather weak determinants and in reality there was much switch between 'moderate' and 'ultra' depending upon circumstances. Indeed, once proportional representation elections were introduced in 1971, it was usually the case that Protestant voters supported parties from both wings of the movement, voting 'moderate' Ulster Unionist Party first, and 'ultra' Democratic Unionist Party second, or vice versa. The divide was far more political than it was social.

It was determined, more than anything, by the perceived demands of the moment.

Unionist fragmentation

We can track the breaking apart of the previously hegemonic Unionist bloc as the redoubt of Stormont crumbled and then collapsed. William Craig's leadership of Unionist hardliners from the beginnings of the civil rights movement crystallized a ginger group known first as the 'Portadown Parliament'. By 1972 this had evolved into Ulster Vanguard. Craig made hair-raising speeches at large Vanguard rallies, amply supported by the (legal) paramilitary, the Ulster Defence Association, where he promised 'liquidation' of the enemy. Arriving accompanied by motorcycle outriders, and delivering his harangues under spotlights, Craig led a suspiciously fascist-looking movement; so, at any rate, was the opinion of both unionist and nationalist critics. In March 1973, Vanguard established itself as an independent party. At the other end of the spectrum, pro-O'Neill unionists found a home in the new Alliance Party of Northern Ireland, formed in 1970, or tried to anchor the left of the Ulster Unionist Party. Brian Faulkner, with customary political poise, attempted to balance the wings, but his was a losing battle.

In 1969 Terence O'Neill was able to block his hated rival from succession to the premiership, but by 1971 Faulkner's time had finally come. Faulkner traded upon his reputation for political nous. He had a name for being the most adroit politician in Northern Ireland and he offered himself to Britain as a man who could talk the language of Westminster and deliver the goods. In a manner familiar to British party politics, he saw his role as that of party manager and political broker. His one steady aim, many felt, was to climb the greasy pole to government power. As Ken Bloomfield, a civil servant who worked closely with him, recalled, Faulkner simply 'loved office'. This gave him a political flexibility unusual in the Northern Ireland context, but also created the impression of an unprincipled careerist. British Prime Minister Edward Heath was impressed with this 'hard-working and dynamic politician' though he realized that he 'was mistrusted by many of his colleagues in the Unionist Party'. Faulkner quickly showed that fancy political footwork for which he was renowned. In 1971 he included a non-Unionist in his cabinet, the Northern Ireland Labour Party veteran David Bleakley, and he offered to the nationalist SDLP a system of parliamentary committees to scrutinize legislation. This at least was a nod in the direction of power-sharing and it enthused some in the opposition ranks. Certainly, Britain was impressed.

On the other hand—and this was a big other—in August 1971 he introduced internment, a decision that was perceived as a general attack upon nationalists and soon painfully disastrous in its consequences. This was the last important Stormont contribution to security policy: it was the British army, primarily, which thereafter sought to contain (while often provoking) spiralling IRA violence. In particular, the Bloody Sunday massacre of January 1972 was its responsibility. Nonetheless, the Stormont government was the sacrificial victim, and Britain introduced direct rule in March 1972. 'When Stormont went we were surprised,' recalled Billy Douglas, an Ulster Unionist. 'Because of something that the paratroop regiment did we in Ulster were shocked that we were to be punished in this way.'

Under pressure from Britain, but also because he genuinely believed he was the best man to broker an agreement to preserve the Union while placating nationalist hostility, Faulkner negotiated the Sunningdale Agreement (1973/4)—a power-sharing devolution government in Northern Ireland, with a cabinet drawn from both unionists and nationalists, and a North–South Council of Ireland. For his pains he was overthrown as Unionist leader by the ruling council of the Ulster Unionist Party. Faulkner's political skills were also his downfall: he was simply not trusted as a conviction politician. As the Revd William Beattie, a member of the DUP, expressed it: 'as always, he will go for the short term and personal interest. And the party loses every time on this sort of thing.' Careerism, too many unionists felt, had led him to make fatal compromises under pressure from London.

Faulkner found himself in 1974 once again as Prime Minister of Northern Ireland, while leading a marginal Unionist Party of Northern Ireland, whose membership was mostly the pro-O'Neill remnants who had been so hostile to him in 1969. They were no protection against the loyalist general strike of May 1974, which brought the Sunningdale arrangement crashing down. The October Westminster elections that same year delivered the *coup de grâce* to the unionism of Faulkner, and indeed Chichester-Clark and Terence O'Neill. The Faulkner Unionists polled even fewer votes than the republican clubs (the political front of the Official IRA). Faulkner retired from active politics in August 1976. He was killed in a horse riding accident the following year.

Ian Paisley, meanwhile, had converted his tiny Protestant Unionist Party into the Democratic Unionist Party (DUP) in 1970, signalling a determination to break up the old Unionist establishment. Paisley was by no means typical of the ordinary Protestant people. He ran his own small Free Presbyterian sect, lambasted alcohol and dancing, castigated the Pope as Antichrist, and indulged in such outré campaigns as that to 'Save Ulster from Sodomy'.

Paisley was no straightforward reactionary, however. Despite his undeniable commitment to the full rigours of Reformation theology, he did not demand a Protestant state. He was not even particularly concerned to restore the old discriminatory order in Northern Ireland. Each reform was to be opposed vehemently, but once conceded it was time to move on. Paisley's aim was to preserve the Union through a militancy of language. This did not shade into an endorsement of loyalist violence, though members of loyalist paramilitaries were inclined to pass the blame for their actions onto his shoulders. Paisley's biblically absolute condemnation of loyalist murders—'just as heinous and hellish as those of the IRA'—should be taken at face value. When he made a half-hearted attempt to restore something like the B Specials by establishing a Third Force in 1981—men on a hillside waving gun licences—this was, as wags observed, a mostly harmless 'Third Farce'.

The attraction of Paisley lay precisely in his personality, as a throwback to an archaic Ulster Protestant evangelical tradition of unyielding hostility to Roman Catholicism and mistrust of British two-facedness. Though he could certainly shift his position for political advantage—opposing and then supporting internment, veering on his attitude to devolution—Paisley came across not just as obdurate but actually uncomprehending of British blandishments and nationalist dissembling. 'I'm not anti-English in the sense that I'm opposed to the English people,' he told an interviewer. 'But I am certainly anti-English politicians—and no doubt about that. I utterly detest them.' At a time when any concession granted under pressure seemed to many Protestants to risk an irreversible slide away from the Union, Paisley's Reformation-inflected rhetoric served as a guarantee against the seductive powers of British blandishment.

In opposition to the Sunningdale Agreement, Vanguard, the DUP, and the majority of the Ulster Unionist Party coalesced into the United Ulster Unionist Council (UUUC). This did not presage a restoration of Protestant unity, however. The fundamental reason for division remained: the tactical conundrum of how the British government was most effectively to be influenced.

Bill Craig (Figure 8), the Vanguard leader who for some time had looked like a more credible, modern alternative to Paisley, exposed his fundamental weakness by allowing mercurial creativity to get the better of him. Already he had coquetted with the idea of

8. **Bill Craig addresses an Ulster Vanguard rally, 1972.**

'negotiated independence' for Northern Ireland. This excited some British commentators, who thought they could detect an emergent Ulster nationalism which, if nothing else, would allow Britain to disengage from Northern Ireland. In reality, Ulster independence was for most Protestants simply a backstop, a way of making it quite clear that British withdrawal would not lead to a united Ireland but rather a disastrous re-partition. Craig, however, was inclined to let his political imagination run away with him. In August 1975, he proposed a 'voluntary' power-sharing agreement with the SDLP, on the British constitutional precedent of wartime National Governments, and he was disowned by his own followers. Vanguard collapsed.

The UUP moved into stagnant waters under the uninspiring leadership of Harry West (1974–9). This was Paisley's moment but he almost blew it by supporting a general strike organized by the loyalist paramilitaries in 1977, which was stoutly resisted and defeated by the British government as a de facto coup attempt. James Molyneaux, leader of the Ulster Unionists at Westminster, declared the UUUC dissolved. Despite the failure of the strike, Paisley's DUP did well in the shortly following local council elections, winning 12.8 per cent of the vote to the UUP's 30 per cent and easily displacing the remnants of Craig's Vanguard as the voice of militant unionism.

Unionist consolidation

By this time it had become apparent that the British government was unwilling to push for any kind of innovative settlement in Northern Ireland. They extended to unionism 'guarantees' that effectively amounted to a veto on radical constitutional reform. For the foreseeable future British government policy was to contain the IRA campaign in the hope that it would eventually run out of steam. Unionists of all shades were broadly happy with this. They united around opposition to any 'Irish dimension', such as a Council of Ireland, and opposition to power-sharing with nationalists.

In theory, the unionist demand was for a restoration of a majority-controlled devolved government in Northern Ireland. This, as well they knew, was a complete non-starter. Britain wanted to avoid stirring the pot in Northern Ireland: handing power over to hard-line Protestants would be ridiculously provocative. But unionists were anxious only to show that they rejected any constitutional innovation. Direct rule was quite acceptable, so long as unionists were in a position to effectively lobby or berate British government policy as the situation required.

The Ulster Unionist Party in 1979 elected as leader James Molyneaux, a tight-lipped, inexpressive politician who cultivated an anti-charisma. He quite openly expressed his disbelief in his own party's formal commitment to the restoration of Stormont. Molyneaux was happy with direct rule, so long as he had the ear of the British government. 'You can fight a lot of ways,' he said, 'by exposing what's going on and especially by exposing to British ministers what's going on.' Molyneaux's appeal was that he was trusted to keep a beady eye on British slippage. Though deeply suspicious of the British establishment, particularly the Foreign Office, Molyneaux thought that Thatcher was sound enough. Paisley continued his tub-thumping, reliably playing his role as a wittily charismatic Cassandra.

Molyneaux, the quiet man who pressed sobering advice on British politicians, and Paisley, the thunderer always on the lookout for betrayal, fought like Kilkenny cats when it came to election campaigns. But in practice they were a double act to maximize unionist pressure on the British government, and Protestant voters responded accordingly, dividing their proportional representation between the UUP and the DUP. Unionism, it appeared by the 1980s, had effectively established a veto not simply on attempts to tamper with partition but on any significant political change at all. This left constitutional nationalism in a bind. While they could condemn the IRA's use of violence as both immoral and politically ineffective, it was not clear that their own commitment to electoralism was any better at delivering substantive reform.

Finding a strategy—the SDLP

While the Unionist bloc had broken up in the 1970s, nationalism came together to dominate the Catholic electorate in the shape of the Social Democratic and Labour Party. As the rather awkward name suggested, however, the SDLP was itself something of an amalgam. It took over the electoral base of the old Nationalist Party by welding together its younger, more vibrant elements with nationalist-labour politicians from Belfast and middle-class civil rights activists centred on Derry. This took some time and the SDLP was only formed in 1971. From the beginning, it was much more a coalition of personal fiefdoms than it was an integrated political formation.

Its nominal leader was Gerry Fitt, Westminster MP for West Belfast. Fitt was enormously energetic and somewhat uncontained, he talked a 'blue streak' as the Irish politician Conor Cruise O'Brien said of him. Fitt formed an unsteady alliance with the truculent socialist Paddy Devlin. Devlin, in 1969, won a Stormont seat for a constituency centred on the Falls Road. At the time, Devlin was formally a representative of the Northern Ireland Labour Party, though he owed his success not to party label but to his civil rights activism, outspoken socialism, and a republican past. His party's election material, nonetheless, was emblazoned with the slogan 'British Rights for British Citizens', an incongruous and not to be repeated species of election-winning propaganda in this strongly nationalist district. Austin Currie and Eddie McGrady came over from the Nationalist Party. But the real counterweight to the Belfast socialists was John Hume in Derry, representative of the 'schoolteachers' wing of the SDLP, and very soon established as the leading strategist of the party. In July 1971, after the British army refused any enquiry into the shooting of two young Derry Catholics, Hume announced a party boycott of Stormont. He did not even consult the SDLP's leader in Belfast.

Gerry Fitt and Paddy Devlin, being old Labour men, were of the view that the national question in Ireland would ultimately be solved by the ameliorative effect of left-wing class politics. They wished the SDLP to position itself as mildly socialist, playing down its nationalism, and believed that a power-sharing government with the unionists would allow for politics to shift from the divisive question of the border to a constructive focus on social and economic policy. Over time, they hoped, sectarian division in Northern Ireland would be softened and ultimately partition could be discussed in a calm and constructive atmosphere.

John Hume's position was no more indulgent of physical force republicanism than theirs—if anything, lacking a personal history of left-wing activism, he was rather more dismissive of populist nationalist shibboleths—but he believed that a serious engagement with Unionism on the national question could not be long deferred. Hume favoured a 'historic compromise': a constitutional settlement in Northern Ireland that would institutionally recognize the Irishness of Northern Ireland's Catholic community while admitting that partition could not be ended without majority approval.

For Fitt and Devlin, therefore, the first aim of the party should be to secure an internal settlement within Northern Ireland based upon a power-sharing devolved government. This would ultimately create the conditions for tackling the national question. So far as Hume was concerned, this was putting the cart before the horse. There could be no stable basis for cooperation between nationalists and unionists until the governing institutions of Northern Ireland recognized the legitimacy of the province's place not only within the United Kingdom but also within the nation of Ireland. For Hume, this meant that any settlement must be within an all-Ireland framework. This 'Irish dimension', Hume thought, should contain at least the potential for a dynamic towards eventual Irish unity, no matter how long it might take, to definitively obviate the justification for armed struggle against partition.

The SDLP leadership kept a united front—barely—in the talks that led up to the Sunningdale Agreement in 1974. Hume insisted that the Council of Ireland was not a welcome additional extra to power-sharing, but absolutely central to its functionality. Gerry Fitt, in contrast, considered the power-sharing government for Northern Ireland to be the real prize. Both wings of the party were prepared to swallow the continuation of internment and an unreformed security apparatus as a price for agreement, unpalatable though that was.

Towards the Anglo-Irish Agreement

With the collapse of Sunningdale, however, the tensions within the SDLP could no longer be papered over and there was a struggle for the party's soul. Fitt was prepared to drop the demand for a Council of Ireland if the unionists could be got to agree to an 'internal settlement' of power-sharing within Northern Ireland. For Hume, this was intolerable: any restoration of government at Stormont was valuable not so much in itself, but as a carrot with which to tempt unionists into negotiations. If they were gifted an entirely internal settlement they would never have any incentive to agree to an 'Irish dimension'. Britain, moreover, would feel comfortable in washing its hands of the Northern Ireland problem, considering it to have been more or less solved. The 'historic compromise' between nationalism and unionism, absolutely necessary in Hume's view to remove the rationale for the IRA's violence, would drift out of sight.

As it happened, the unionist majority after Sunningdale was entirely unwilling to negotiate power-sharing—they were quite happy with direct rule—and when Bill Craig contemplated it, as we have seen, his political career imploded. In this context, Fitt's amenability seemed little more than obsequiousness and his reputation rapidly eroded (republicans unkindly called him 'Fitt the Brit'). In 1979 he resigned from the SDLP's leadership—and from the party itself—in a cloud of mutual recrimination.

That year, John Hume finally became the formal leader of the SDLP; but he had been its de facto statesman for some time. The SDLP party conference approved overwhelmingly a call for the British government to end its guarantee to unionists that Northern Ireland would remain part of the United Kingdom so long as a majority wished it, and called on the British and Irish governments to instead work towards an 'agreed Ireland'. Hume used the SDLP as a platform from which to remorselessly repeat, with little variation, his analysis of the situation. Only agreement 'on the island of Ireland' could promote 'peace on our streets'. It was an endlessly recycled and boring mantra, but Hume's calculated aim was to hammer on until he had changed the language of political discourse. First and foremost, he was intent on defining unionism as a problem to be dealt with by the British and Irish governments.

It remained the case that the unionists had very little reason to seriously negotiate with the SDLP. The British government was not prepared to apply serious pressure on the unionists to concede either power-sharing or an Irish dimension. Hume, therefore, concentrated on building relations with the Irish political establishment in the hope that momentum could be built from that end. He was a key mover in the establishment of the New Ireland Forum of 1984, which brought together all the constitutional nationalist parties on the island of Ireland to agree a common position (Sinn Féin was excluded; unionists were invited but declined to attend). The Forum proposed three models for settlement: Irish unification, Irish Federation, and joint British/ Irish sovereignty over Northern Ireland. These were tartly rejected by Thatcher. The real importance of the Forum, however, was in its definition of the problem. 'For nationalists,' its report insisted, 'a central aim has been the survival and development of an Irish identity, an objective that continues in Northern Ireland today as nationalists seek effective recognition of their Irish identity.'

The nationalist argument was that by refusing to coercively intercede between the parties in Northern Ireland, Britain had effectively given the unionist majority an absolute veto on any important political change. When the issue was precisely one of the legitimacy or otherwise of the state, this was a dereliction. Catholics were understandably 'alienated' from the institutions of state. Only government-led activism, forcing unionists to make substantive concessions, could hope to advance the situation. Hume was disgusted at British abdication. 'I...believe that the perennial British view of the problem as "their quarrel" and "not ours" is fundamentally wrong: Britain is, in fact, included in the quarrel as a central protagonist, and must be centrally involved in the solution.' To a considerable extent, the British government ultimately adopted this analysis; not so much by dint of argument, more because of the rise of Sinn Féin after the hunger strikes of 1981. This disconcertingly demonstrated that nationalist alienation provided a ready reservoir for violent disaffection.

With the shifting of Britain's position, the unionist double act—Paisley's blustering belligerence and Molyneaux's 'masterful activity'—was reaching the end of its utility. Anglo-Irish talks from 1980 ramped up in 1984, eventuating in the Anglo-Irish Agreement of 1985. This effectively reversed what had up until that point been seen as the natural sequence for any settlement. An 'Irish dimension' was introduced in the form of compulsory rights of consultation for the Irish government regarding any matter affecting the interests of the nationalist minority in Northern Ireland. This applied to everything within the competence of the Secretary of State for Northern Ireland, who ran the direct rule administration. It meant continuing direct rule, but with a distinctly green tinge.

The process and the result of the Anglo-Irish Agreement made painfully obvious to unionists that they had been sidelined. They could only hope to restore their influence on the government of Northern Ireland by agreeing to devolution, and this would only be available at the price of agreeing to power-sharing with nationalists and a new form of Irish dimension. The Anglo-Irish Agreement, therefore, was not a settlement of the Northern Ireland problem—nor was it intended to be—but a means by which to create a dynamic in which unionists, for the first time since Sunningdale, would be under pressure to seriously negotiate.

The immediate response, however, was massive unionist rejection of the Anglo-Irish 'diktat'. They recognized just how dangerously novel the Anglo-Irish Agreement actually was in giving the Irish government rights of consultation:

> The right to interfere, to persuade, to pressurise at the highest level, enforceable by International Law, plus an obligation on the British to attempt compromise, are weapons of immense potential, particularly when granted to a state in respect of a territory it claims as its own.

Boycotts, rallies, and the resignation of parliamentary seats to trigger simultaneous by-elections as a de facto plebiscite on the Agreement were effective at displaying the fury of Northern Ireland's Protestant community. But as the institutions of the agreement were intergovernmental, based on the Dublin–London axis, it could not be brought down from within Northern Ireland. In the view of the Irish Taoiseach who negotiated the agreement, Garret FitzGerald, the ultimate positive achievement of the Anglo-Irish Agreement was to convince nationalists that Britain was at last prepared to face down unionist obstructionism: 'nationalists accepted the agreement overwhelmingly... due not so much to the many changes produced by the agreement... but rather to the scale of unionist protests against the agreement, which convinced the nationalist population that it represented a major step forward'. Unionists fumed, but it gradually dawned on them that their only way out was through negotiation.

Towards the political process

It is not immediately apparent, however, that unionists had anyone to negotiate with. Almost as soon as the Anglo-Irish Agreement was relatively stabilized, Hume turned to talks with the leadership of Sinn Féin and the IRA. Hume felt that Sunningdale had failed partly because it had been attempted with IRA violence in full swing. A comprehensive 'historic compromise', he felt, would have its best chance if the republican movement could be brought on board. Hume's own party, the SDLP, was painfully aware that Hume's reaching out to republicanism threatened to undermine their own legitimacy as the authoritative voice of the nationalist community. But for Hume, the SDLP was an instrument for bringing about the historical compromise, and its longer-term viability or even existence was dispensable to this greater goal.

The Anglo-Irish Agreement demonstrated to the unionist mind that the double act of Paisley's loud belligerence and Molyneaux's quiet lobbying was no longer adequate. They had been manoeuvred into a position where they had to consider how to negotiate. The priority now was to draw lines in the sand and to protect them. This was not an easy process.

Molyneaux eventually resigned as leader of the Ulster Unionist Party in 1995, to be succeeded by David Trimble, a former supporter of Vanguard and academic lawyer who offered un-illusioned and sternly unsentimental attention to brief and detail. He would negotiate the new dispensation. Paisley and the DUP preferred to remain offside. In 1996 a Forum was elected to provide political parties with an up-to-date mandate for negotiations. The most successful parties were the Ulster Unionist Party, the SDLP, the DUP, and Sinn Féin. The newly formed Northern Ireland Women's Coalition won only two seats out of 90, with 1.03 per cent of the vote. Nonetheless, there was a great deal for a specifically female voice to contribute. Mo Mowlam, the Labour Secretary of State, remarked that women were an underappreciated but crucial constituency in the peace process:

> It is impossible to quantify, but the contribution of individual women and women's groups to the cause of peace in N. Ireland is immense. Across all communities, the links and relationships that women forge in the work that they do—usually away from the public gaze—has been invaluable in keeping the social fabric of N. Ireland together, especially in the most troubled times....The women in the talks were a real positive force.

Nonetheless, the male domination of the political class at this time is striking.

There unfolded a tortuous and prolonged twin track: a peace process, seeking to lure Sinn Féin away from the 'armed struggle', and a political process, in which the SDLP and Trimble's UUP hammered out a power-sharing settlement. As it transpired, progress was possible because the SDLP felt it could go relatively easy on the 'Irish dimension'. The Anglo-Irish Agreement was already there as a backstop which would come into effect every time devolution was suspended and replaced by direct rule from London. Because of the peace process, absent during Sunningdale, the Irish dimension could be considerably 'domesticated' to the institutions of Northern Ireland governance itself, through radical reform of the security forces and the public sphere. The end result was the Belfast or (as nationalists preferred) Good Friday agreement of 1998. The SDLP and the UUP had reached a 'historic compromise'. It won both Hume and Trimble the Nobel Peace Prize, and destroyed the leading political role for their respective parties.

Chapter 5
The twenty-first century

The Good Friday Agreement saw considerable institutional restructuring in Northern Ireland. An Assembly was elected in 1998, with women constituting 14 per cent of its 108 members. The Ulster Defence Regiment had already been transformed in 1992 into the Royal Irish Rangers, a much less problematic military formation. The Royal Ulster Constabulary was renamed the Police Service of Northern Ireland and, in a measure requiring derogation from British anti-discrimination legislation, a quota was established for Catholic recruitment so as to make it for the first time more or less representative of the Northern Ireland population. Operation Banner, the British army deployment in Northern Ireland, was formally wound up in July 2007. A power-sharing government, with David Trimble as First Minister and Seamus Mallon of the SDLP as Deputy First Minister, operated between 1998 and 2001.

So far as the primary negotiators of the Good Friday Agreement were concerned, this was a settlement built to last. For the Democratic Unionist Party and Sinn Féin, however, it had a rather different status. The DUP opposed the agreement as giving too much away. Their intention was to weaken its all-Ireland dimension. Sinn Féin, curiously enough, shared a similar aim. They did not wish to see the agreement consolidated as an indefinite arrangement for the governance of

Northern Ireland. Rather, they saw it as a mechanism by which the party could build itself as the hegemonic force in northern nationalism and a substantial presence in politics south of the border. They wished to see the agreement as transitional to a situation where the unification of the island would be a possibility.

The republican movement did little to allow David Trimble, leader of the Ulster Unionist Party, to sell the agreement to his followers. Though it was passed by referendum, as the capstone of peace, it did not win Protestant hearts. The IRA was exceptionally slow to decommission its arms, and this meant that the stabilization of a power-sharing government proved very difficult. Between 2001 and 2007, the power-sharing government collapsed. This did not, however, mean a collapse of the peace process. The expectation was always that the government would be restored and the struggle now was over which parties would dominate when it did.

Both the DUP and Sinn Féin succeeded in becoming the main political parties for their respective communities. The DUP had little difficulty in accusing Trimble's party of canoodling with terrorists. Sinn Féin was able to capitalize on the 'whiff of cordite' from the long years of the Troubles. As Danny Morrison, close to the Sinn Féin leadership, put it,

> …the SDLP continues to be viewed as the soft underbelly of nationalism…It is no accident that Sinn Féin is viewed by its supporters and opponents alike as tough and tenacious. Those qualities distinguish it from the SDLP and those qualities emerged from republican ideology and aspiration, experience of oppression, struggle and resistance, long years of imprisonment, the reading of history.

Those who declined to vote for the armed struggle would, nonetheless, vote for a party that had steeled itself in the conflict.

Ian Paisley, for his part, saw an opportunity to at last, after decades, take control of unionism in Northern Ireland. Of deep and unyielding religious convictions himself, and long dependent on a Free Presbyterian hard-core, Paisley had always known how to work with allies from the more secular wing of unionism. The hard-headed lawyer Desmond Boal had helped him to establish the DUP back in 1970. Now the party was opened up for those increasingly frustrated at Trimble's attempts to pivot simultaneously against the extremes on both sides. The Ulster Unionist Party had come near to collapse by 1974 only to be welded together again by the 'masterful inactivity' of James Molyneaux. Trimble's hyperactivity served to open up these divisions again. 'Within the Ulster Unionist Party there was a sort of fractioning post Belfast Agreement,' Peter Weir remembered; 'effectively it created two parties'. In January 2004, the prominent MP for Lagan Valley, Jeffrey Donaldson, defected from Trimble's party to the DUP and he was joined by other luminaries of the UUP new generation, including Arlene Foster. The long-delayed disintegration of the UUP's leading role, often challenged but uninterrupted since 1905, had come to pass.

The extremes came together in an agreement to reconfigure the 1998 settlement. The St Andrews Agreement, negotiated in Scotland in 2006, settled a path for the decommissioning of IRA arms (these were not handed over to the British). To general amazement, Ian Paisley became First Minister and Martin McGuinness Deputy First Minister in May 2007. McGuinness was to remain in place for almost ten years while Paisley was succeeded first by Peter Robinson, then by Arlene Foster.

This says something about the nature of the two political parties. In reality, DUP supporters had never been against any kind of compromise under any conditions. Rather, they did not trust the available political leaders not to be inveigled by conniving nationalists and haughty British politicians. On the other side, the percentage of Catholics who would settle for nothing less than an imminent United Ireland was always quite low. They recognized Sinn Féin's cadre ideology as a means to an end—maintaining a vanguard and a principle—rather than the stuff of immediate practical politics.

Identity politics

Both Sinn Féin and the DUP saw merit in that their own unconquerable wills finally represented their communities and in this they won quite broad agreement from their respective electorates. Neither believed that a definitive settlement had really been achieved. For the Democratic Unionist Party, politics was about holding the line against further incursions on the Union. For Sinn Féin, it was all a matter of maintaining a momentum, with a united independent Ireland as an inevitable terminus. Politics characteristically focused around cultural issues determining the extent to which Northern Ireland could be considered fundamentally British or fundamentally Irish. It was a struggle over the appropriate equilibrium for 'parity of esteem' between the two communal blocks. Social and economic innovation by the power-sharing government was not entirely lacking—there was at least some movement to peg back the socially inegalitarian and archaic 11+ system—but such matters took a decidedly second place. Britain remained sovereign, but rather distant, and practical all-Ireland institutions virtually invisible.

As the armed conflict faded into history, there were interesting shifts in ethnic identities in Northern Ireland. There emerged a 'Northern Irish' identity, which placed accommodation within the constitutional balance of Northern Ireland above identification with either Britain or Ireland as such. The Northern Irish identity, which was adopted by around 25 to 30 per cent of the population, in roughly equal numbers by both Catholics and Protestants, was primarily attractive to young urbanites. It was a self-conscious reaction to the perceived aridity of communal politics. It was also, however, a rather fluid construction. Catholics would drift towards the designation when the reformist momentum in Northern Ireland appeared to be strong. Protestants were more likely to adopt it as a red line when they felt under pressure from Irish 'cultural contamination' of the province.

The 'Northern Irish' identity was of particular significance because, after a long period of stability, demographic change was again becoming a powerful force in Northern Ireland. The 2011 census showed that self-described Catholics now made up 45 per cent of the population while the Protestant proportion had fallen to 48 per cent, for the first time a minority. Amongst schoolchildren, the change was even more drastic, with 51 per cent Catholic and 37 per cent Protestant. A Catholic majority in the population by the time of the 2021 census seemed likely. This was a remarkable change from the traditional one-third/two-thirds divide in Northern Ireland and was mostly to be explained by differential rates of emigration. This did not mean, however, that a United Ireland was inevitable. As ever, many if not most Catholics opposed any such leap in the dark and while the anti-unionist identities of Catholics remained strong, their Irish identity competed with Northern Irish, occasionally British, or simply a preference not to prioritize any such label.

Nonetheless, in the context of an increasing Catholic population percentage in Northern Ireland for the first time in a generation, a united Ireland by consent within a foreseeable timeframe became a real political prospect. The negotiators of the 1998 Good Friday Agreement had hoped to establish a framework which would, in practice, last indefinitely. They had been succeeded by political forces, however, which were much more inclined to look upon the present dispensation as provisional. Sinn Féin sold itself as the party which would maintain momentum and keep a united Ireland on the medium-term agenda. The Democratic Unionist Party, on the contrary, increasingly represented itself as the party which would defend the ethnic interests of the Protestant population in Northern Ireland. Certainly they did not abandon hope that the Union could be maintained indefinitely but there was an acknowledgement that this would require continual movement and adjustment. What was lacking in Unionism, however, was a genuine assimilatory optimism that Catholics could be reliably converted *en masse* in favour of the union. The politics of working-class loyalism were perhaps the most overtly pessimistic.

For unionists, 'parity of esteem' was not just irritating because it licensed expressions of Irish identities in Northern Ireland which, in their view, were offensively associated with republican paramilitarism. Perhaps more worryingly, it demoralized Protestants and encouraged a higher emigration rate out of the province. Commemoration (Figure 9) in particular remained a

9. An early monument erected in the republican bastion of south Armagh commemorating fallen IRA Volunteers. Such monuments proliferated in the 21st century.

fraught topic. Hundreds of plaques and monuments to those who died in the Troubles peppered Northern Ireland. Few were ever seen simply as commemorating a victim: most were seen as political appropriations of victimhood for political purpose. There was erected, for example, a memorial at Claudy, commemorating the horrific IRA bomb attack of 1972. It depicted a young girl—the 8-year-old Kathryn Eakin—kneeling in pain, holding her hands to the side of her head. In 2007 the monument was seriously vandalized. 'This wasn't casual vandalism,' her mother said. 'It took a lot of effort. It has to have been planned.' The dead could not be easily laid to rest. There was no agreement on establishing a 'Truth Commission' to agree a narrative of the Troubles and each revelation of security force collusion with loyalist paramilitarism reopened bitter wounds.

In many respects, Northern Ireland settled into a not entirely happy deadlock, but one which was much preferable to the traumatic years of the Troubles. Nationalist energy, now focused through Sinn Féin, was to a large extent redirected south of the border. An important reason for adopting the peace strategy for Sinn Féin had been the low ceiling the IRA had imposed upon its potential vote in the republic. Gerry Adams, president of Sinn Féin, in 2011 won a seat in the Irish Dáil, leaving the secondary work of operating the Northern Ireland government to his deputy, Martin McGuinness. Sinn Féin, indeed, did make considerable headway, reaching 13.8 per cent of the vote in the republic's general election of 2016. Its aim was to find itself in government on both sides of the border. How this might in itself advance the cause of Irish unity was never made clear, but the important thing for Sinn Féin was to have a strategy of advance. So long as this was in place, it could fairly easily see off the cavils of rejectionist republican hardliners. The DUP, for its part, saw its role as more defensive. With a devolved government back in place in Northern Ireland, relatively secure from capricious interference by the British government, the old unionist priority of maximal unity came back into play. The economic sovereignty of the Northern Ireland government was extremely limited and as might be expected culture remained the primary battlefield. The DUP laboured incessantly to prevent any further Hibernicization of Northern Ireland under the rubric of 'parity of esteem'.

The DUP worked hard to maintain the adhesion of working-class unionism which, in a disturbing drift of nomenclature, came to be termed 'loyalism' (for most of the Troubles this had been a term used exclusively to label the assortment of Protestant paramilitaries). Morale was not high amongst working-class Protestants. Traditionally, working-class Protestant communities had been led by a well-paid, highly skilled, trade unionized, and self-confident industrial 'aristocracy of labour'. They had been proud of their work discipline and strong values. In the 1980s, this had been described by a Protestant worker from Londonderry's Waterside district:

> The Protestants are proud, a very proud people, and most of them would like to think that they're a cut above everybody else, above the Catholic community. They keep down their families (the size of the family), they have lovely homes—they try to have a lovely home, a nice home. They don't seem to care how well their children get on in their education, but when I say they've got a lovely home—social climbers just.

The uncertainty was already evident here, and as Northern Ireland deindustrialized the structures of Protestant working-class culture entered into full crisis.

Protestant Ulster was justifiably proud of the province's industrial legacy. Protestants tended to view Catholics as deficient in their work ethic, though a 1978 survey found remarkably similar outlooks between Catholics and Protestants in their attitude to work. As Ken Heskin, a psychologist, put it, 'The Protestant ethic is alive and well and living in the Falls Road!' The generation born around the time the Troubles began had, as children, demonstrated a striking realignment of life experience. In 1981, as Jean Whyte found, 12-year-old children in Catholic west Belfast scored higher in terms of self-esteem, social intelligence, confidence in the future, and positive attitudes towards education than their counterparts in Protestant east Belfast. By 2017/18, only one of the top ten best schools in Northern Ireland was Protestant, the rest were Catholic. About 50 per cent more Catholics than Protestants were entering higher education. With the introduction of Fair Employment legislation in 1989, which for the first time seriously tackled discrimination in private employment, and more importantly with the mighty shipbuilding industry and ancillary industries downsizing to little more than tourist heritage, the balance of economic advantage in the new services economy began to disproportionately benefit Catholics rather than Protestants.

Working-class loyalist culture felt left behind (and in so doing identified with elements of the working class in Great Britain who were increasingly turning to politics of the populist hard right). A decision in 2012, in the spirit of 'parity of esteem', to cease flying the British flag over Belfast City Hall on a continuous basis led to a succession of angry and mostly working-class street protests by Protestants bitter at the loss of their cultural favour. Increasingly, the DUP felt that it had to draw a line against any further encroachment by cultural nationalism. In particular, dispute came to focus upon a proposed free-standing legislative Act to promote the Irish language.

Sinn Féin was worried that its core support felt that it was making too many compromises in the North to facilitate its advance in the South. The DUP, for its part, feared that it was losing the hearts and minds of the Protestant working class. The involvement of DUP ministers in a baroque scandal over subsidies for clean energy, which quickly turned into a 'get rich quick' scheme for those in the know, was the final trigger. In January 2017, Sinn Féin withdrew from the power-sharing government and it again collapsed. Britain declined to reintroduce direct rule formally, though the Northern Ireland Office continued to function under its direction, so that by 2019 Northern Ireland held the world record for the longest period for a region without any government. In 2020, the political parties finally met to painfully reassemble devolved government.

The aggressive masculinity of social relations in Northern Ireland, most likely buttressed by decades of political violence, was reflected by a shockingly high rate of 'domestic' murder in the province, equalling that of Romania. Nonetheless, the twenty-first century—finally—saw a notable if still inadequate feminization of the political class (Figure 10). Sylvia Hermon, widow of Sir Jack Hermon, Chief Constable of the RUC, was elected to the Westminster constituency of North Down in 2001 as an Ulster

10. A republican mural celebrates the female contribution to their struggle. Women are depicted banging bin lids, a common tactic in the 1970s to warn IRA Volunteers of approaching army raids, and protesting in favour of the 'blanket protest', the refusal to wear convict uniform, at Armagh Women's Prison.

Unionist. She resigned the party whip in 2010 and as a notably liberal Independent increased her vote in subsequent elections. Her ability and popularity were equally evident. Naomi Long, leader of the moderate Alliance Party, astonished political opinion by winning the East Belfast Westminster constituency from Peter Robinson, leader of the DUP, in 2010. She lost the seat five years later, but remained a high-powered political presence. In January 2015, Julie-Anne Corr Johnston, aged 27, was elected as a Belfast City councillor for the Progressive Unionist Party, the small political wing of the UVF. She was openly lesbian. This was a remarkable and remarkably progressive development in loyalist politics. At the end of 2015, Arlene Foster became the first female leader of the DUP, a sharp contrast to that party's historically rather traditional view of gender roles. In February 2018, Gerry Adams finally stood down as leader of Sinn Féin. He was replaced as all-Ireland party leader by Mary Lou McDonald, while Michelle O'Neill was elected leader of the party in the North. Karen Bradley, admittedly unimpressive in her ignorance of Northern Ireland, was made Secretary of State in January 2019. The change in the public face of the political class in Northern Ireland was dramatic and widely appreciated. It indicates well that the national question in the province is not simply an atavistic throwback. The contenders in the dispute have always looked to don the mantle of modernity at least as much as the robes of tradition.

Northern Ireland and Europe

As so often in Northern Ireland, British political considerations impacted as an exogenous shock with the Brexit referendum of 2017. For the scholar Brendan O'Leary, this demonstrates a perennial and ever-destabilizing reality for the province: 'conflict and conflict-resolution are shaped from outside, not just within'. Northern Ireland, as a depressed region of the European Union, generally benefited from European largesse, though it was much smaller than the money-pump from London. Most importantly, for nationalists, membership of the European Union was a supranational identity which softened the border within Ireland and diminished the ultimate sovereignty of Britain. While in Britain there was a considerable amount of working-class rebellion against the status quo expressed in an anti-membership vote, Northern Ireland Catholics of all classes were massively in favour of remaining within Europe. Working-class Protestants cleaved more closely to the British model and their somewhat exaggerated and rather insular Britishness looked much less out of step with the political and cultural norms of Great Britain than had previously been the case. However, as in Britain, a certain middle-class and cosmopolitan British identity favoured membership of the European Union. Northern Ireland as a whole voted against Brexit, despite the largest single party—the DUP—being enthusiastically pro-Exit.

When Theresa May's Conservatives were denied a majority by a resurgent Labour Party in the June 2017 general election, a pact was negotiated between the Conservatives and the DUP to keep the former in power. For the first time in over a century, the leadership of the Conservatives began again to stress the 'Unionist' in the title of their party. The British government wished itself to be seen as an honest broker between the political forces in Northern Ireland. Its open alliance with the DUP put this under enormous strain.

The Northern Ireland question became a massive issue in the negotiations to disentangle the United Kingdom from the European Union. The Irish government during the referendum campaign had dropped its normal policy of refusing to take sides in the domestic affairs of Great Britain in order to argue for the United Kingdom to remain within the European Union. They feared both the impact of Brexit on their own economy and the destabilization of the situation in Northern Ireland. After the referendum, Ireland launched an impressive diplomatic campaign to prevent the re-emergence of a 'hard border' in Ireland, using the Good Friday Agreement as a lever to this end. It succeeded both in rallying other European member states behind the principle and forcing the United Kingdom to accept that a hard border was not acceptable.

For unionists in the North, withdrawal from the European Union was attractive in that it would restore British sovereignty as the ultimate basis for Northern Ireland. For nationalists, however, the crisis also had an appeal in that it reinforced the idea that Northern Ireland, which had voted for remain, was a place apart from Great Britain, with interests and a popular will at odds with that of England and Wales, and converging with that of Ireland. Unionists contemplated the alluring prospect of Northern Ireland standing proudly with the United Kingdom as it stepped out on the world stage as a completely independent sovereign state. Nationalists felt that Ireland, supporting and supported by the European Union community of nations, compared well to an insular and reactionary United Kingdom increasingly dominated by English nationalism. That Great Britain had, in its public mind, moved on from the Northern Ireland Troubles was evidenced both by the visible irritation most Conservatives had for the Irish border question as a spoke in the wheel of Brexit, and the lack of traction, for good or ill, of Labour leader Jeremy Corbyn's long history of sympathy for the republican movement in Northern Ireland.

British politics became obsessed with the 'Northern Ireland Backstop', a mechanism to ensure that the all-Ireland economy, seen as foundational to the Good Friday Agreement, would be preserved. This would mean Northern Ireland remaining within the EU customs union and closely aligned to the single market. It was, as traditional in Northern Ireland, a polarizing issue: 98 per cent of Sinn Féin and SDLP supporters backed it compared to only 27 per cent of Ulster Unionist Party supporters and 5 per cent of DUP supporters. It did, however, have a great deal of pragmatic backing from business and agricultural interests.

This is unsurprising. Even as late as the 1990s, the standard of living in Northern Ireland had been considerably greater than that in the republic, while taxes were lower and social spending more substantial. Northern Ireland, however, was something of a dole economy, kept afloat by the British Exchequer. Public spending in Northern Ireland as a percentage of regional GDP hovered at around 60 per cent by the 1980s and reached an astonishing 73 per cent in 2009. As a flexibly sovereign economy, within the market discipline of the European Union, the republic leapt ahead in the 1990s. True, southern Ireland's headline figures benefited from the creative accounting of multinationals nominally located in the country for tax purposes. But the underlying dynamism of the economy was undeniable. Even after the grievous impact of the 2008 Great Recession on the independent Ireland, a mere 71,000 of the island's 324,000 entrepreneurs resided in Northern Ireland. Ulster was no longer the capitalist leader of Ireland. The Republic of Ireland, long a bastion of conservative Catholicism, 'modernized' at breakneck speed from the 1990s. Even with its social inequalities and injustice, Ireland became an icon for liberal and neoliberal dynamism in an era of otherwise morbid capitalism. A largely working-class and youth revolt against the iniquities of Irish capitalism, with social services unacceptably poor and house prices and rents absurdly high, combined with a consciousness of the unfulfilled promises of independence highlighted by a decade of centenary commemorations. This powered an extraordinary breakthrough for Sinn Féin in the February 2020 southern Irish elections. Sinn Féin soared to become the largest single party in the state by popular vote, winning almost a quarter of the total, and easily the largest party on the island of Ireland. It was a signal triumph; and yet another dramatic twist in the Irish gyre.

Since the agreement, it had proven surprisingly easy to make the border more or less invisible. Real work had focused on accommodations within Northern Ireland and between the islands of Great Britain and Ireland. The Brexit crisis made it once again a live issue, but to a large extent the prospect of physical checks on the border was something of a red herring. The issues at stake were much more profound. For nationalists the border was not one with a foreign country. Northern Irish nationalists resented Britain telling them that any part of their Ireland was alien. The island stood on the brink of being psychologically repartitioned, or, conversely, and to unionist horror, partly reunited if Europe's economic border came to run down the Irish Sea. The stakes were higher than they had been for decades. Ireland found itself wrestling once again with the perilous British question. When the crunch came, in the autumn of 2019, Britain proved itself once more a perfidious ally for the unionists, plumping for a withdrawal agreement that placed a soft economic border down the Irish Sea rather than at the border.

Paramilitarism, meanwhile, was by no means completely effaced. A joint report issued in October 2015, drawn up by the Police Service of Northern Ireland and MI5, concluded that all the main paramilitary groups that had been active during the Troubles continued to exist, to recruit, and to have a relatively prominent public profile in the life of Northern Ireland. While this was seen as a risk to national security, it was admitted that all the groups, the Provisional IRA included, were committed to peaceful progress towards their political objectives, and there was a strong sense in which their continued existence, though illegal, was useful because 'they played an important role in enabling the transition from extreme violence to political progress' by maintaining discipline and solidarity amongst their followers. Lashing out by loyalists and anti-peace process activities by hard-line republican dissidents remained a formidable threat, however.

In April 2019, during a series of police raids on the Catholic and deprived working-class Creggan district of Derry, the so-called New IRA fired at police officers. A journalist (and gay rights activist), Lyra McKee, who was standing near the police, was shot and killed. The public reaction was strong against this reversion to the politics of violence. As so often in Northern Ireland, tragedy combined with fear and hope as people absorbed the grim fact of another political fatality.

Conclusion

Small nation separatism has its benefits, certainly. But the fragmentation of multinational and multi-ethnic states, which encourage a politics predicated on socio-economic distribution and interest, building bridges across ethnic and cultural lines, implies a grievous loss. In Ireland, at any rate, the theoretical loss need not be so narrowing. In principle, and often in practice, the unionist ideal of a multinational United Kingdom is enlarging and noble. In principle, and often in practice, the nationalist ideal of an expanded 'cross-community' Ireland—by which the UK would 'lose' only about 3 per cent of its population, but Ireland would 'gain' nearly 30 per cent in its citizenry—is also enlarging and noble. Neither tradition in Ireland need be seen as inherently insular or a turning away from others. Most noble of all, of course, is an enduring politics of freedom, toleration, and ambition across these islands, however constitutionally organized.

The Good Friday Belfast Agreement had succeeded in drawing a line under the worst of the violence of the Troubles but it was also a signpost to an uncertain future. The most reliable solvent of ethnic division in modern society, class politics, remained liminal in Northern Ireland, not least because it is generally in retreat elsewhere. As time goes on, the zero-sum politics of identity, culture clash, and flag-waving—the politics that for a long period seemed to mark Northern Ireland out as unusual and even pathological—increasingly becomes a defining characteristic of 21st-century capitalism. In the future, Northern Ireland might well suffer not just from exogenous shocks, but even more perilously an exogenous environment of right-wing nativist populism. Perhaps Northern Ireland has learnt tough lessons that will help it avoid the perils that come into view across much of the world. History need not be wasted. But while the 1998 Agreement should be recognized as a triumph of peace-making, it would be unwise to take any of this for granted. The dynamics of polarization have been attenuated but not eliminated. History has not reached a final destination in the province.

Glossary

Catholic In Northern Ireland those born into a culturally catholic and generally nationalist community. Historically, active identification with the Roman Catholic faith has tended to be high, but as an ethnic group, Catholicism was as much a social and political identity as it was specifically religious.

constitutional parties During the Troubles a term applied to political parties and movements which disavowed the use of lethal illegal violence, whether the party in question supported current constitutional arrangements or not.

direct rule Governance of Northern Ireland without any intermediary local devolved government. In practice, the governing Northern Ireland Office was usually run from London at arm's length.

gerrymandering A term taken from American politics, where the practice is frequent, of manipulating constituency boundaries in order to ensure the electoral security of one party. Gerrymandering was generally used to unionist advantage.

loyalists Before partition a term generally synonymous with unionists. By the late 1960s it generally referred to unionist ultras hostile to the relatively moderate Ulster Unionism of Terence O'Neill. During the Troubles it most often referred to those sympathetic to or supportive of the Protestant-based pro-British paramilitaries whether illegal (e.g. the Ulster Volunteer Force) or legal (until 1992, the Ulster Defence Association). In the 21st century the term has come to be applied to disaffected working-class unionists more generally.

Loyal Orders Unionist and Protestant mass organizations which gather to process with music on particular commemorative dates, such as 12 July. Most important is the Orange Order and the Apprentice Boys of Derry.

nationalists Those in favour of a united and independent Ireland at least as an ultimate ideal. The Nationalist Party of the Stormont era reflected this politics and the SDLP is often referred to as nationalist. While it does not exclude republicans it is generally assumed that the centre of gravity of 'nationalism' eschews political violence.

Northern Ireland Often referred to as Ulster, particularly by unionists, though it comprised only six of the nine counties of the historic province of Ulster.

'one man, one vote' The most resonant slogan of the civil rights movement that broke out in 1968. Specifically, it referred to the restrictive ratepayers' local government franchise, but also alluded to the deficiencies of representation for Catholics as a result of both gerrymandering and discrimination.

Protestants Adherents to those churches which identify with the Reformed Christian faith, in Northern Ireland most importantly the Anglican Church of Ireland and the Presbyterian Church in Ireland. Theological divisions between the Churches only served to reinforce the important ethic of freedom of conscience and religious liberty that underpins the unionist political vision.

republicans Those in favour of a united and independent Ireland as a priority and as soon as practicably possible. During the IRA's armed campaign the term was generally understood as referring to those who supported the IRA or other similar armed groups (e.g. the Irish National Liberation Army).

southern Ireland The most common vernacular designation of the independent state formally known, in English, as 'Ireland'. Nationalists are unhappy at the implication that Ireland might be complete without the six counties of Northern Ireland; unionists resent the implication that Ireland has a moral right to the territory of the entire island.

Stormont The seat of the devolved government and parliament in Northern Ireland. The term is generally deployed as synonymous with the Unionist government of Northern Ireland between 1921 and 1972 (though the Stormont buildings were not opened until 1932).

the Troubles A term used to refer to sustained and violent civil disorder in Ireland since the 1920s. It usefully distinguishes between simple militant protest and full-scale civil or international war. From quite early, about 1971, it became the default term for the crisis in Northern Ireland. Its end is usually identified with the second IRA ceasefire of 1996.

unionists Those in favour of the union between Ireland, later Northern Ireland, and Great Britain within a sovereign United kingdom. When the term is capitalized, it often refers to members of the Ulster Unionist Party.

Volunteer A term used by paramilitaries to refer to their members. Government, and those hostile to the aims of the paramilitary in question, would generally use the term 'terrorists' or 'men of violence'.

Sources and further reading

Introduction

David McKittrick, Seamus Kelters, Brian Feeney, and Chris Thornton, *Lost Lives: The Stories of the Men, Women and Children who Died as a Result of the Northern Ireland Troubles* (Mainstream: Edinburgh, 1999).

Frank Burton, *The Politics of Legitimacy: Struggles in a Belfast Community* (Routledge and Kegan Paul: London, 1978), p. 63.

E. E. O'Donnell, *Northern Irish Stereotypes* (College of Industrial Relations: Dublin, 1977), pp. 96–101.

Richard Rose, *Governing without Consensus: An Irish Perspective* (Faber and Faber: London, 1971), p. 216.

Dr Raymond McClean, *The Road to Bloody Sunday* (Poolbeg Press: Dublin, 1983), p. 141.

Poll: '51% of people in Northern Ireland support Irish unification, new poll finds', <https://www.thejournal.ie/lord-ashcroft-irish-unification-poll-4804372-Sep2019/>.

Chapter 1: The origins of the Troubles

William Makepeace Thackeray, *The Irish Sketchbook* (Charles Scribner: New York, 1848), pp. 394–5.

Fenian quotation: *Report of the Special Commission, 1888* (HM Stationery Office: London, 1890), pp. 116–17.

Benedict Kiely, *Counties of Contention* (Mercier Press: Cork, 1945), p. 178.

Cahir Healy, speech in Stormont, 24 April 1934, in Gerard Reid (ed.), *Great Irish Voices: Over 400 Years of Irish Oratory* (Irish Academic Press: Dublin, 1999), p. 256.

Patrick A. Macrory, *Review Body on Local Government in Northern Ireland* (1970), Cmnd 546.

Denis Barritt and Charles F. Carter, *The Northern Ireland Problem: A Study in Group Relations* (Oxford University Press: Oxford, 1962, 1972), p. 108.

Victor Griffin, *Mark of Protest: An Autobiography* (Gill & Macmillan: Dublin, 1993), p. 90.

William A. Carson, *Ulster and the Irish Republic* (William W. Cleland: Belfast, 1956), p. 38.

Cardinal William Conway: G. W. Tagart, *Unholy Smoke* (Hodder & Stoughton: London, 1969), p. 80.

Chapter 2: The government

Petrol bombers liable to be shot: *The Times*, 3 April 1970.

Michael Dewar, *The British Army in Northern Ireland* (Arms and Armour: London, 1986, 1995), p. 47.

Robin Eveleigh, *Peace Keeping in a Democratic Society: The Lessons of Northern Ireland* (C. Hurst & Co: London, 1978), p. 61.

Maudling on Protestant backlash: Reginald Maudling, *Memoirs* (Sidgwick and Jackson: London, 1978), pp. 180 and 184.

General Tuzo's concerns: John McGuffin, *The Guineapigs* (Penguin: London, 1974), p. 44.

John Peck, *Dublin from Downing Street* (Gill & Macmillan: Dublin, 1978), pp. 3–4.

The Cecil King Diary, 1965–1970 (Jonathan Cape: London, 1975), 4 April 1972, p. 194.

Cabinet would 'carefully consider' an all-Ireland referendum: Mike Garnett and Ian Aitken, *Splendid! Splendid! The Authorised Biography of Willie Whitelaw* (Jonathan Cape: London, 2005), pp. 137–9.

British officials consider IRA demands as an 'opening bid': TNA PREM, 15/1009, Note for the Record, 7 July 1972.

Whitelaw on Motorman: William Whitelaw, *The Whitelaw Memoirs* (Aurum Press: London, 1989), p. 105.

Michael McKeown, *The Greening of a Nationalist* (Murlough Press: Lucan, 1986), p. 114.

Army dragging its feet over UWC strike: Robert Fisk, *The Point of No Return: The Strike which Broke the British in Ulster* (André Deutsch: London, 1975), pp. 87–8.

Letter from Heath to David Bleakley: David Bleakley, *Peace in Ireland* (Mowbray: London, 1995), p. 120.

Austin Currie, *All Hell Will Break Loose* (O'Brien Press: Dublin, 2004), p. 275.

Merlyn Rees on 'Ulster Nationalism': Merlyn Rees, *Northern Ireland: A Personal Perspective* (Methuen: London, 1985), pp. 21, 93, 99, 107.

Ulster Housewife: Richard Rose, *Northern Ireland: A Time of Choice* (Macmillan: London, 1976), p. 95.

Sir Frank Cooper: Thomas Hennessey, *The First Northern Ireland Peace Process: Power-Sharing, Sunningdale and the IRA Ceasefires, 1972–76* (Palgrave Macmillan: Basingstoke, 2015), p. 169.

Merlyn Rees, *Northern Ireland: A Personal Perspective* (Methuen: London, 1985), p. 49.

Soldier in South Armagh: A. F. N. Clarke, *Contact* (Martin Secker & Warburg: London, 1983), pp. 109–10.

'…a punch here, a kick there': Bernard O'Mahoney with Mick McGovern, *Soldier of the Queen* (Branson: Dingle, 2000), p. 200.

Roy Mason, *Paying the Price* (Robert Hale: London, 1999), pp. 165–6.

James Prior, *A Balance of Power* (Hamish Hamilton: London, 1986), pp. 181–2.

Thatcher on Irish 'folklore': Garret FitzGerald, *All in a Life: An Autobiography* (Gill & Macmillan: Dublin, 1991), p. 506.

New Ireland Forum Report (The Stationery Office: Dublin, 1984): <https://cain.ulster.ac.uk/issues/politics/nifr.htm>.

The Alastair Campbell Diaries: Volume 2, Power and the People, 1997–1999 (Hutchinson: London, 2011), p. 14.

Chapter 3: Paramilitarism

Evelyn Sharp, *Unfinished Adventure: Selected Reminiscences from an Englishwoman's Life* (Faber and Faber: London, 1933, 2009), p. 216.

John McKeague, speaking about the violence of August 1969 in Rosita Sweetman, *'On Our Knees': Ireland 1972* (Pan Books: London, 1972), p. 230.

Terence O'Neill, *The Autobiography of Terence O'Neill* (Hart-Davis: London, 1972), p. 66.

Shane O'Doherty, *The Volunteer: A Former IRA Man's True Story* (Fount Paperbacks: London, 1993), p. 27.

IRA Volunteers psychologically normal and with republican relatives: Patrick Bishop and Eamonn Mallie, *The Provisional IRA* (Corgi: London, 1988), pp. 13–15.

Joe Cahill: Brendan Anderson, *Joe Cahill: A Life in the IRA* (The O'Brien Press: Dublin, 2002), p. 207.

Seán Mac Stíofáin, *Memoirs of a Revolutionary* (Gordon Cremonesi: Edinburgh, 1975), p. 208.

'…place at a conference on the future of Ireland': Maria Maguire, *To Take Arms: A Year in the Provisional IRA* (Quartet Books: London, 1973), p. 69.

Seán Mac Stíofáin, *Memoirs of a Revolutionary* (Gordon Cremonesi: Edinburgh, 1975), p. 286.

Maria Maguire, *To Take Arms: A Year in the Provisional IRA* (Quartet Books: London, 1973), p. 126.

Loyalist News: Morris Fraser, *Children in Conflict* (Secker and Warburg: London, 1973), p. 118.

'Romper Room': John Black, *Killing for Britain* (Wolfhound Press: Dublin, 2008), pp. 367–8.

Justice Lowry: Anne Cadwallader, *Lethal Allies: British Collusion in Ireland* (Mercier Press: Cork, 2013), pp. 306–7.

Army document on 'decent people': 'Operation Playground', September 1972, Appendix 2 in Roger Faligot, *Britain's Military Strategy in Ireland: The Kitson Experiment* (Brandon and Zed Press: London, 1983), p. 216.

'…babes in arms': Quoted in Norman Lockhart's report in Peace by Peace, October 1976, reproduced in Rhoda Watson (ed.), *Along the Road to Peace: Fifteen Years with the Peace People* (Community of the Peace People: Belfast, 1991), p. 19.

Peace People dissenters: Richard Deutsch, *Mairead Corrigan, Betty Williams* (Barron's: New York, 1977), pp. 152–5.

Middle-class Andersonstown: Pat Walsh, *Irish Republicanism and Socialism* (Athol Books: Belfast, 1989), p. 125.

Nell McCafferty, *Peggy Deery: A Derry Family at War* (Virago: London, 1989), p. 106.

Sally Belfrage, *The Crack: A Belfast Year* (Grafton: London, 1988), p. 328.

Opsahl Inquiry: Andy Pollak (ed.), *A Citizens' Inquiry* (Lilliput Press: Dublin, 1993), p. 316.

IRA on 'Long War': *Republican News*, 9 December 1978, in Brian Hanley, *The IRA: A Documentary History, 1916–2005* (Gill & Macmillan: Dublin, 2010), p. 189.

Bobby Sands, 'Training Camp' in Bobby Sands, *Writings from Prison* (Mercier Press: Cork, 1998), p. 216.

Judith Ward, *Ambushed: My Story* (Vermilion: London, 1993), pp. 91–2.

Sister Sarah Clarke, *No Faith in the System: A Search for Justice* (Mercier Press: Cork, 1995), p. 178.

Dáithí Ó Conaill in Padraig O'Malley, *The Uncivil Wars: Ireland Today* (Beacon Press: Boston, 1983), p. 273.

Gerry Bradley with Brian Feeney, *Insider: Gerry Bradley's Life in the IRA* (The O'Brien Press: Dublin, 2009), pp. 222–3.

Danny Morrison: Eamonn Mallie and David McKittrick, *Endgame in Ireland* (Hodder & Stoughton: London, 2000), p. 68.

Chapter 4: The political parties

Kenneth Bloomfield, *Stormont in Crisis: A Memoir* (Blackstaff: Belfast, 1994), p. 221.

Edward Heath, *The Course of my Life: My Autobiography* (Hodder & Stoughton: London, 1998), p. 426.

Billy Douglas: David Hume, *The Ulster Unionist Party, 1972–92* (Ulster Society: Lurgan, 1996), p. 46.

Revd William Beattie: W. H. Van Voris, *Violence in Ulster: An Oral Documentary* (University of Massachusetts Press: Amherst, 1975), p. 306.

Paisley anti-English politicians: Padraig O'Malley, *The Uncivil Wars: Ireland Today* (Beacon Press: Boston, 1983), p. 185.

James Molyneaux: Padraig O'Malley, *The Uncivil Wars: Ireland Today* (Beacon Press: Boston, 1983), p. 160.

Gerry Fitt: Diary entry for 28 June 1970, reproduced in Conor Cruise O'Brien, *States of Ireland* (Panther: Bangalore, 1974), p. 211.

New Ireland Forum Report (The Stationery Office: Dublin, 1984): <https://cain.ulster.ac.uk/issues/politics/nifr.htm>.

John Hume, *Personal Voices: Politics, Peace and Reconciliation in Ireland* (Town House: Dublin, 1996), p. 57.

Unionist view of Anglo-Irish Agreement: Peter Smith, *Why Unionists Say No* (1985): <https://cain.ulster.ac.uk/events/aia/smith85.htm>.

Garret FitzGerald, *Just Garret: Tales from the Political Front Line* (Liberties Press: Dublin, 2010), p. 374.

Mo Mowlam, *Momentum: The Struggle for Peace, Politics and the People* (Hodder & Stoughton: London, 2002), p. 233.

Chapter 5: The twenty-first century

Danny Morrison, 'The Real Slow Learners', 21 June 2004, in Danny Morrison, *Rebel Columns* (Beyond the Pale: Belfast, 2004), p. 70.

Peter Weir: Jonathan Tonge, Máire Braniff, and Thomas Hennessey, *The Democratic Unionist Party: From Protest to Power* (Oxford University Press: Oxford, 2014), p. 27.

Claudy monument: Susan McKay, *Bear in Mind These Dead* (Faber & Faber: London, 2008), pp. 334–3.

'Derry Man—Waterside', in Peter McNamee and Tom Lovett, *Working-Class Community in Northern Ireland* (Ulster People's College: Belfast, 1987), p. 457.

Ken Heskin, *Northern Ireland: A Psychological Analysis* (Gill and Macmillan: Dublin, 1980), p. 50.

Jean Whyte, *Changing Times: The Challenge of Identity: 12 Year Olds in Belfast, 1981 and 1992* (Avebury: Aldershot, 1996).

Domestic violence: 'Femicide: The murders giving Europe a wake-up call' (7 September 2019), <https://www.bbc.co.uk/news/world-europe-49586759>.

Brendan O'Leary, *A Treatise on Northern Ireland*, 3 vols (Oxford University Press: Oxford, 2019), III, p. xiv.

'Paramilitary groups in Northern Ireland' (October 2015), A Report for the Secretary of State, p. 2: <https://www.gov.uk/government/publications/assessment-on-paramilitary-groups-in-northern-ireland>.

Index

For the benefit of digital users, indexed terms that span two pages (e.g., 52–53) may, on occasion, appear on only one of those pages.

Northern Ireland

GEOPOLITICS
A Very Short Introduction
Klaus Dodds

In certain places such as Iraq or Lebanon, moving a few feet either side of a territorial boundary can be a matter of life or death, dramatically highlighting the connections between place and politics. For a country's location and size as well as its sovereignty and resources all affect how the people that live there understand and interact with the wider world. Using wide-ranging examples, from historical maps to James Bond films and the rhetoric of political leaders like Churchill and George W. Bush, this Very Short Introduction shows why, for a full understanding of contemporary global politics, it is not just smart - it is essential - to be geopolitical.

'Engrossing study of a complex topic.'

Mick Herron, Geographical.

SCOTLAND
A Very Short Introduction
Rab Houston

Since Devolution in 1999 Scotland has become a focus of intense interest both within Britain and throughout the wider world. In this Very Short Introduction, Rab Houston explores how an independent Scottish nation emerged in the Middle Ages, how it was irrevocably altered by Reformation, links with England and economic change, and how Scotland influenced the development of the modern world. Examining politics, law, society, religion, education, migration, and culture, he examines how the nation's history has made it distinct from England, both before and after Union, how it overcame internal tensions between Highland and Lowland society, and how it has today arrived at a political, social and culture watershed.

Houston's survey is clear and certainly concise.

Clare Beck, The Scotsman

www.oup.com/vsi

CATHOLICISM
A Very Short Introduction
Gerald O'Collins

Despite a long history of external threats and internal strife, the Roman Catholic Church and the broader reality of Catholicism remain a vast and valuable presence into the third millennium of world history. What are the origins of the Catholic Church? How has Catholicism changed and adapted to such vast and diverse cultural influences over the centuries? What great challenges does the Catholic Church now face in the twenty-first century, both within its own life and in its relation to others around the world? In this Very Short Introduction, Gerald O'Collins draws on the best current scholarship available to answer these questions and to present, in clear and accessible language, a fresh introduction to the largest and oldest institution in the world.

www.oup.com/vsi

CHRISTIAN ETHICS
A Very Short Introduction
D. Stephen Long

This *Very Short Introduction* to Christian ethics introduces the topic by examining its sources and historical basis. D. Stephen Long presents a discussion of the relationship between Christian ethics, modern, and postmodern ethics, and explores practical issues including sex, money, and power. Long recognises the inherent difficulties in bringing together 'Christian' and 'ethics' but argues that this is an important task for both the Christian faith and for ethics. Arguing that Christian ethics are not a precise science, but the cultivation of practical wisdom from a range of sources, Long also discusses some of the failures of the Christian tradition, including the crusades, the conquest, slavery, inquisitions, and the Galileo affair.

www.oup.com/vsi

SOCIAL MEDIA
Very Short Introduction

Join our community

www.oup.com/vsi

- Join us online at the official Very Short Introductions **Facebook** page.
- Access the thoughts and musings of our authors with our online **blog**.
- Sign up for our monthly **e-newsletter** to receive information on all new titles publishing that month.
- Browse the full range of Very Short Introductions online.
- Read **extracts** from the Introductions for free.
- Visit our library of **Reading Guides**. These guides, written by our expert authors will help you to question again, why you think what you think.
- If you are a teacher or lecturer you can order inspection copies quickly and simply via our website.

ONLINE CATALOGUE
A Very Short Introduction

Our online catalogue is designed to make it easy to find your ideal Very Short Introduction. View the entire collection by subject area, watch author videos, read sample chapters, and download reading guides.

http://fds.oup.com/www.oup.co.uk/general/vsi/index.html